FIVE YEARS'

IN A
COUNTRY PARISH

BY THE
RECTOR OF RUSPER
THE REV. EDWARD FITZGERALD SYNNOTT M.A.

COUNTRY BOOKS

Published by Country Books
Courtyard Cottage, Little Longstone, Bakewell, Derbyshire DE45 1NN
Tel: 01629 640670
e-mail: dickrichardson@country-books.co.uk
www.countrybooks.biz
www.sussexbooks.co.uk

ISBN 978-1-906789-96-1

British Library Cataloguing in Publication Data.
A catalogue record for this book is available from the British Library.

ACKNOWLEDGEMENT:
*My thanks to The Rev. Nick Flint, Rector of Rusper,
who kindly made his copy of the original book available
to me and supplied the photographs.*

FRONT COVER PICTURES:
Rusper Church and The Rev. Edward Fitzgerald Synnott

TITLE PAGE PICTURE:
The Rev. Edward Fitzgerald Synnott

Printed and bound in England by:
4edge Ltd., Hockley, Essex. Tel: 01702 200243

CONTENTS

A FOREWORD

When I accepted the living of this tiny parish of Rusper—which is a quaint old village on the eastern edge of Sussex—some of my clerical and lay friends pronounced themselves very envious of me.

They assured me that after my twelve years of strenuous work for the Church in and around London, in Devonport, in Worthing, and in Canada, I deserved the placid life I was about to enjoy.

That was just five years ago — five terrible years! How often during those five years of agony have I wished that, instead of succumbing to the lure of a quiet, rural parish, I had declined the living and pursued the happier and more strenuous life to which I had been accustomed!

I remember in particular the rosy picture of my future that was drawn for me by one of my friends. He placed me in a sheltered rectory, over which the golden honeysuckle climbed. My flock were to be a few good-hearted rustics, who would greet their rector with a doff of the hat or an old-fashioned curtsey. Squire and gardener, peasant and artisan, would welcome me as their friend, their guide, and minister. Instead of writing my sermons under the flickering gaslight of a London slum, I would prepare them in blissfully ideal surroundings — while sauntering through God's green fields or wandering down fragrant, shady lanes.

The music of the birds would harmonise with my own care-free soul; for all would be joy and song within me.

So spoke my friend, interpreting perhaps the thoughts of most people who reflect upon the life of a village rector.

How different has been the picture from the reality! Exactly how different I can never adequately tell. When Queen Mary died she spoke of Calais being graven on her heart; when I die I think that the name of Rusper will be found eaten deep into mine.

Though I bear malice towards none, yet in justice to my Church, to other clergymen who are suffering or may endure something of what I have experienced, to my wife and daughter who have shared my sorrows, and to myself, I feel I must describe in all their terrible realism some of the agonising experiences through which I have passed.

I shall show how the idle and thoughtless tittle-tattle of a small village can grow and spread until the first feeble untruth in which it begins assumes a shape so ugly and alarming that the daily life of a parish priest becomes a burden almost unbearable. I shall show how every mannerism, every gesture, every modern thought, every unusual word or act of a man with an up-to-date and original mind, every suggestion of muscular Christianity which would pass unnoticed in a town or city, or be counted to him for righteousness, can be made the subject for village gossip and criticism leading to the ruin of the rector and his family.

After the most careful deliberation, I have decided to tell to the whole world my remarkable story.

CHAPTER I

RUSPER'S CALL

R usper! Five years ago the number of persons who had heard of the village was very small. Now, through the revelations of the life that goes on in this place — revelations that I and others were compelled to make at my trial before the Consistory Court — this obscure hamlet is known in every corner of the kingdom

Rusper has become a byword! It is a synonym for slander, backbiting, and gossip, and as such it will probably appear in the standard English dictionaries of the future.

For many years of my active life the average country living held very few attractions for me. But I had often said to my wife that if I ever accepted a country living it would be Rusper. (I never sought Rusper. It sought me. To my great surprise, I received a letter one evening in February, 1914, asking if I would consider the offer of the living. The patroness of the living, the late rector's sister, expressed the view of her deceased brother, whose last wish was that I should be offered Rusper. The parish needed a strong man, and I. was the strong man selected for the work!

I was not unknown to Rusper. As far back as 1908 my predecessor asked me to preach there for Dr. Barnardo's Homes, and each year until 1914 I delivered the annual sermon at the church. I decided to accept the offer of the living.

It was on June 22nd, 1914, that I came into residence. I had looked forward to the day as one of the red-letter days of my life. Everywhere I had been a success. In my youth I was in the

Royal Irish Constabulary. I spent six of the happiest years of my life in this magnificent force. I won prizes in those days as an athlete; I competed in all forms of sport, football, swimming, fives, and boxing. I was champion boxer in the Royal Irish Constabulary for several years, and during this time I fought hundreds of hard-won fights. Then I came to London, studied for the Church, took my degrees, and became, in 1898, curate of St. Michael's, Southfields. After that I went on to St. Matthias', Surbiton, in 1900, and in ten weeks the church was filled. And so on! Wherever I went, the congregation grew. I never preached to empty pews, and when I said farewell to one church I was invariably presented with tokens of esteem to which the whole congregation subscribed. I write these things, not in a spirit of boasting, but to show the great contrast between the life at an average town or city church and that of a tiny village church, where gossiping is the chief social interest.

Later I went to Devonport as chaplain to Sir John Jackson's employees at the great harbour of Keyham; again I left with tokens of esteem to which over two thousand people had subscribed, and it was after working for Dr. Barnardo's Homes in the dioceses of Chichester and Winchester for seven years that I decided to make the eventful change.

I saw no earthly reason why I should not be as successful in Rusper as I had been elsewhere. During the last few years when slander — the sword of the coward that has cut many a throat by a whisper; that poisoned arrow shot in the dark — was knocking at my door; when each morning brought a new sensation to whip me into desperation, I wonder that I did not take the wings of the morning and fly to the uttermost parts of the earth.

I envied the cattle grazing in the fields, I longed for their quiet life; I envied the dog his life in the street; I envied the shepherd folding his flock of sheep. Daily the feelings of a man who was being hunted for some great crime grew upon me. The days of the week were all the same. True, Sunday brought a slight change — but not for the better. Then I had to present a smiling face to my congregation — to some who I knew were doing their best to ruin me.

Especially during the last two years did the cloud darken my home, and take the light from my eyes so that I became oblivious of the passage of the seasons. For two years I did not see the sun, moon, or stars. I knew the seasons when I broke the ice on the water for the cattle to drink. I knew it was seed-time when my faithful foreman came and awoke me from my stupor and told me so. I knew it was summer when I stroked the horses I loved as they plodded round the fields to the whirr of the mowing-machine. Even now I feel as one awaking from an evil dream.

In the old classic, Horace tells us that when the Creator made man he took a particle from one place and a particle from another until the whole was blended into a man. Then he took a particle of a lion and put it into a man's heart. Often has this thought helped me — when I forgot, in moments of spiritual darkness, that I was a minister and priest — that I was, at any rate, a man, and had that little bit of a lion in my heart.

Rusper in 1905 from the Knight Album. Little had changed when Synnott arrived in 1914

CHAPTER II

I ARRIVE

Coming to Rusper was like entering a lovely garden, only to be blindfolded and marched over a terrible precipice. I remember well the golden day in June when I saw my late residence at Worthing empty of the last piece of furniture; how I harnessed my lovely cob "Kitty" and secured my faithful dog "Pat" in the trap. Kindly neighbours were at the door to wave me an affectionate farewell.

It was a twenty-seven miles' drive to Rusper. "Kitty" had often done fifty miles in a day, so she took her task kindly. "Kitty" was fond of eggs, which were cheap in those days. She took a dozen of them, new laid, in a quart of milk, and followed with ten pounds of oats. We made the twenty-seven miles' journey in three hours and ten minutes.

These two friends, "Pat" and "Kitty," were soon lost to me. "Pat" was "slandered" very early. One morning when he was tied up in the kitchen, he was supposed to have crossed the path of a cyclist who was thrown, and who, unfortunately, died the same evening. I heard that my innocent "Pat" was blamed for the accident, but my surprise was great and my sorrow greater when "Pat" disappeared shortly afterwards. Later his tail was sent to me through the post, and I then knew that he had suffered at the hands of a local executioner.

"Kitty," too, departed. I had to part with her to obtain the funds wherewith I successfully defended my honour. Soon I had but one animal friend left, my dog "Bob," whose life for a time was also in danger.

When I arrived at Rusper, my wife, who had travelled by motor-car with my daughter and a maid, had been in the village for several hours. After grooming my pony and kissing her "good-night," I went into the rectory and drank a cup of coffee. To my surprise the hard water had turned the coffee and milk to curdles. Was it a symbol of the cup of sorrow I was to drink during the coming five years?

One of the drawbacks of this village is the water-supply. Although the Surrey main is only five hundred yards away, red tape and Bumbledom have kept the water out of the parish. There is, of course, the village pump. But, like the United States, it has gone dry, and the villagers must get their supply of water from what is popularly called the "dip-ponds," where cattle leisurely wade in summertime.

I have been indebted to friends for my supply of drinking water, although on one occasion I was even refused water by a parishioner who had plenty and to spare. When I have handed the chalice of our redemption at the Holy Communion, and when those lips that touched and drank from that chalice have been used to send a message that my invalid wife could have no more water, I have remembered the words of our Lord: "A cup of water in My name!"

On the morning following my arrival at Rusper, I received a message from the gardener saying that twenty-one of the chickens that I had brought from Worthing had been stolen during the night — my first night in the village! Ye gods! One would have thought I should have been given a chance to turn round and buy a padlock. A parishioner called the same morning and said that he knew there were thieves about, as the hair had been cut from his horse's tail, and his cattle had been turned into the road during the night.

This turning of cattle into the road, where they are likely to be the cause of terrible motor-car accidents, appears to be a favourite pastime in Rusper. Some of the persons who do this have even had the temerity to telephone the police and acquaint them with what has been done.

These early losses were but the beginnings of my misfortunes. The living of Rusper is worth only £180 a year net. I was receiving more than this when I accepted the living, so that, unlike the call of many of the cloth, which is to a higher salary, I was called to a lower paid position. I came to Rusper without counting the cost. I was then worth some thousands of pounds; to-day I possess nothing. Until I came to this luckless place, everything that I touched turned to gold. To-day I could not produce a pound were I asked to do so.

Chapter III

RUSPER'S DIVES AND LAZARUS

I shall never forget my impressions when I faced my first congregation in Rusper.

I had often read of the tyranny of the countryside, and I recall how one of my tutors once told me that he preferred the meagre salary of a college professor to an opulent living in a country parish, where the big houses — the big purses — ruled the church, the incumbent, and the congregation, making life insufferable to the parish priest.

The big purses were very much in evidence on that first Sunday morning. They sat in their cushioned pews, wearing their silks and fine raiment, and listened to my sermon with an air of critical superiority.

Some of the wealthy families represented that morning — as I have since learned — have for years ruled the parish with all the exactitude of the laws of the Medes and Persians, ever with the cry of unity and more unity, which always meant the predominance of the "Big Party." I noticed with pain the superior attitude adopted by some of these families to the rest of the congregation; and I determined that, come what might, I would be as outspoken in my criticism of the shortcomings and sins of the wealthy families as of the sins of the unfortunate poor.

I decided that one of my first sermons should be based on the grand and simple teachings contained in the Sermon on the Mount. I spoke of the great ideals of poverty, humility, turning of the other cheek, self-sacrifice, loving our enemies, innocence and purity. I was prepared for criticism from the opulent section of my congregation — in fact, I was anxious for it, so that I might talk to one and the other exactly as I felt as their guide and minister; but I was not prepared for the deluge of objections that enveloped me.

What did I mean by daring to suggest that it was sinful to roll in luxury and to spend a life of idleness? Did I mean that it was a sin to own a motor car? Did I want to make Rusper a hotbed of Socialism? Did I think that they should pay their workmen what they asked? Did I not know that the poor could not handle money if they received it; that they would only waste it and want more? Did I not believe in any class distinctions, or was I just rhapsodising? And so on.

I feel sure that some of my wealthy parishioners have never yet forgiven me for that sermon, and for daring to preach a grand ethical code in a place where money was the god that ruled and was worshipped.

Some went so far as to urge me to drop preaching. Sermons, said they, were not wanted. Why was I not content with services only? These were the days when people preferred ritual to orations. I told them bluntly that since I did not believe that Christianity was a splendid hypocrisy, I proposed to preach and to say what was in my mind, irrespective of the wealth or influence of those who disagreed with me.

I continued to draw harsh pictures of the millionaire who called himself a Christian, and proceeded to rub in the text: "How hardly shall they that have riches enter the Kingdom of Heaven." I criticised the politician who called himself a Christian, but was trying to serve God and Mammon. I criticised the smart leaders of Society, who also claimed to be good Christians, while despising and disdaining the poor of their own district. I dwelt upon the spectacle of the labourer eating his scanty dinner, while the opulent landlord regaled himself with choice dishes.

This style of preaching may hold fashionable West End congregations, keen on Society sensations; but in a country village, where it is equally needed, it has, as I soon found, a very different reception.

Yet how could I, whose duty it was to preach to my people the word of God as I understood it, hesitate to tell the blunt, though unwelcome truth? I knew that I was offending some of the Dives in my congregation, but I was resolved that I would not be frightened from my task. It was my duty. If I had not done so, if I had moderated my language, I should have been false to my calling and unfit for my post.

While I saw people around me at the zenith of opulence, I saw many more in the depths of poverty. To the full-flushed millionaire religion is an easy garment to wear.

The result of my preaching was soon manifest. The few Dives who composed the principal part of the early congregations presently disappeared from their cushioned pews, and Lazarus and his relatives crowded my little church to overflowing.

Interior of Rusper Church 1905 from the Knight Album

Chapter IV

RUSPER AT HOME

I had not been many days in Rusper before I made my first call on each of my parishioners. It took me a week to do the whole parish, for there are about six hundred residents. Of this first tour I have many vivid recollections. It was a week of gossip, of scandal and back-biting. The unpleasant taste of that first week is still in my palate. Recollections of that tour fill me with doubts about the future of humanity. I feel doubtful whether the race will ever advance to that stage of charity and tolerance when it will see the best as well as the worst in man; when it will cease to malign and begin to praise; when it will sympathise with human weaknesses and believe there is some good in all.

I found that most of my new parishioners were firmly convinced that Rusper was the worst village in England; that but for themselves — who were the modern Mr. and Mrs. Lot in the English Cities of the Plain — there was no good anywhere.

The clergy who had preceded me for two generations, they said, were unworthy of the cloth; leading Churchmen were gamblers, drunkards, or moral degenerates; landlords were usurious; farmers did not pay their rents; tradespeople were rapacious, and customers were debtors; all men and women were living double lives!

At the first house I called I found that I had stepped deep into the unsavoury gossip of the village. As I progressed from house to house, the tide of gossip and scandal rose higher and higher, until, at the end of the week, it seemed to me that this picturesque old village was the last resort of all that was unsavoury and worst in humanity.

I had not been two minutes in the house of the parishioner on whom I first called before I was warned against calling next door. This neighbour, I was assured, was up to her eyes in debt. She was a designing woman. Her daughters, when they were not doing church work in Rusper, were away in London, where they spent their days and nights in gambling-hells.

It is, I believe, a custom to change such a subject without giving the parishioner to understand what is in the clerical mind. I preferred to state quite bluntly that I came to the parish as the minister to all, whatever their failings, and I proposed to call on good and bad alike. In fact, I intended to call oftener on the evil than on the good, so that I might proffer them the spiritual assistance of which they surely stood in greater need. This attitude, I soon learned, put me beyond the pale in this and many another gossiping home.

I called on the next-door neighbour who had been so badly maligned, and found, as in truth I expected, a family of simple, God-fearing people. Then I proceeded further with my visitations. I discovered there were many village feuds as ancient and bitter as some of the feuds which exist among the bluest blood in the land.

The village was full of Pharisees, who smote their breasts and thanked God, and informed me that they were not as other people. And then they proceeded to tell me how the other people differed from their high standard until I grew weary and ashamed.

From cottage I went to mansion, and back again to cottage. I called on the publican and the sinner, the church-goer and the infidel. I entered the village bar and talked with the "lads of the village" who gathered there. When later I called on the Pussy-foot section, I discovered that they had learned that I had crossed the threshold of a public-house, and they expressed themselves as though I were an emissary from the lower regions.

I entered the homes of Dives, who warned me that some of their neighbours were social outcasts, and if I called on them I should be running the risk of being myself cold-shouldered.

"Your predecessor called there, and lived to regret it," said they. "So we hope that you will have nothing to do with those people."

I inquired what was the sin they had committed, and they told me that over twenty years ago they had transgressed the social code. I said that if the transgression had been committed only yesterday, and that if I knew that it would be repeated tomorrow and all the days I spent in the parish, it would not prevent me from doing my duty. I should call on all, irrespective of their social record.

I called on Nonconformists as well as on churchgoers; on the gaol-bird as well as those who called themselves the elite of the parish. One of the parishioners I visited, I remember, was in tears. She had recently married, and her husband had received a communication from an unknown source making cruel allegations against his wife. This poor woman was only one of many who were quietly suffering in Rusper because of the idle gossip or malicious slanders circulated by persons who did not realise or did not care what terrible tribulations they were causing.

Another girl was in great distress because her people had been informed that she had been turned away from her school for smoking and swearing. I saw the woman who was circulating the story, and I saw the girl's school-teacher, and asked her if it were true. When the school-mistress repudiated the story, I went back to the woman who had circulated it and told her that it was her bounden duty to go back to all the people to whom she had communicated it and tell them that it was untrue, but I never heard of her doing so.

At the end of my tour I went for a quiet walk, and I said to myself that if these people say such things of their neighbours, who are not much in the limelight, what are they likely to say of me and my household, who, in a village of this size, are necessarily in the full glare — a magnificent target for all the gossipers in Rusper?

I resolved that I would fight the gossip-mongers tooth and nail. When I met them in the street, and they began to tell me of their neighbours' shortcomings, I asked them plainly, what about the mote in their own eye? I gave a five-minute lecture to one lady upon the necessities of minding her own business. She walked into her house in high dudgeon.

When I made my second call at some of the houses, I was received very coolly. Some, who had warned me against visiting their neighbours, carried their resentment so far as to omit to invite me inside. Others, who occupied some of the big houses, sent back a servant to say that they were out. I heard them giving these instructions while I was waiting in the hall or drawing-room.

Gossip was already beginning to impede my ministrations.

CHAPTER V

FRIVOLOUS CHARGES

I came to Rusper because the people of the parish fancied they wanted a strong man. I soon found they really wanted a jelly fish — one who would adapt himself and his ideas to all the strange, old-fashioned notions which had been inherited from their great-grandmothers.

There is an old saying that if you want to keep your friend, don't tell him of his faults. Some of my congregation were only too ready to come to me with the latest gossip of the village about myself.

I started to make a catalogue of some of the allegations that these malcontents made against me. I find in this list such imaginary crimes as the following:

My voice lacked the melancholy tone.
I sang too loudly.
I was not a good timekeeper.
I did not cross myself.
I paced through the service like a man about to catch a train.
I let the children fall when I baptised them.
I pinched them to make them cry.
I put the wedding-ring on a lady's thumb.
I married the wrong people.
I hurried them through the burial service, and did not give the bearers sufficient time to lower the coffin.
I pronounced the solemn words, "Ashes to Ashes," before I took my stand at the grave.

The greatest offence of all was that I left bread on the Holy Table, and thus sinned against the Holy Ghost. This offence was made known not only in the parish, but from Horsham to Three Bridges.

For ages theologians have puzzled their brains to arrive at a satisfactory solution of what is meant by sinning against the Holy Ghost, and yet in Rusper amateur theologians were quite ready to make a pronouncement upon this difficult text.

I endeavoured to teach my congregation that reverence is purely relative. What is reverence to one is irreverence to another. The Jew sits down to preach; the Anglican stands up. The Anglican kneels to pray; the Presbyterian stands.

When I learned of all these strictures being passed upon myself, I recalled what had been said to me of my predecessor before I came to the parish, and my soul went out in sympathy towards him. None will ever know, as they know of me, what that man of God must have endured.

Six years before I came to Rusper as its rector, I visited the village, and was met by one of the pillars of the church at that time. His words made an indelible impression on my mind. They seemed completely devoid of the Christian charity that one had a right to expect from a member of the Church.

"I am glad to see a new face," said he. "We are tired of our old parson. I have written several letters to the Bishop about him, and we have held meetings to get him moved on. But he stays on for the sake of the loaves and fishes."

Loaves and fishes they were, in very truth! There was not much left for luxury foods from a salary of less than four pounds a week, with rates and taxes and many other expenses to meet.

This practice of writing to the Bishop, to which I have already referred, seems to be regarded as a strictly correct proceeding in Rusper, and some of my congregation, I believe, make a habit of it.

So far as I was concerned, it had begun before I entered into residence. Consequently, the Bishop sent for me, and asked me concerning some of the objections that had been raised. One of these objections, I discovered, was that as I had been seven years out of parochial work, I had lost my skill in the cure of souls.

23

I reminded the Bishop that I was licensed by him seven years previously, that I had worked in the diocese and was well-known, that I had been offered the living of Rusper, and as I was eligible to fill it, no one could keep me out of it.

CHAPTER VI

TYPES IN MY CONGREGATION

If I had searched England I could not have found a congregation containing more remarkable and eccentric types of humanity. I once preached a sermon to my congregation upon themselves. I called it "The People in the Pews." For many it was the first time that they had seen themselves as others saw them.

Some of them grew red in the face, shuffled their foot, and twisted and turned in their seats; they opened their prayer-books and closed them again, glanced all round the church, looking at everyone but the preacher. Yet none of them rose to leave until after the service was ended.

I have catalogued some of these types. First in the list I place the lady scribes.

These are the worshippers who bring their notebooks, and write down for their diaries any unusual thing that they may see or hear. Many of these do this from the highest motives. They record any great and lofty thought, any telling quotation, or a moving stanza from the poets that I may have quoted in my sermon, and carefully treasure these for reference during their private meditations. Such a practice I welcome and would like to see extended.

But I soon found that others were actuated by different desires. Some of the "gossipers" use these notebooks to record trivial departures from the usual, to be retold and exaggerated over the telephone on the following morning, or at dinner-parties, or sewing meetings.

One or two of these lady scribes manifest a keen interest in

25

the habiliments I wear. Their notebooks contain entries stating that the colour of the stole I wore on a certain Sunday was different from that which the diarist considered should be worn. These "sartorial" ladies discovered that I had worn blue or red or white, when they expected me to wear green. As a matter of fact, the colours that I wear are never irregular. The explanation is quite simple, and I would have been pleased to tell them if I had known what was their difficulty. Actually I was wearing the sequence as prescribed by the old Sarum code, instead of the colours in more common use.

I cannot help feeling very sorry for persons who can become so interested in their clergymen's habiliments as to write a description of them in their diaries. I must give these "sartorial" ladies credit for being themselves very punctilious as to their own apparel. They are invariably gowned in a prim and puritanical style. To them Paris and her fashions make no appeal. The fashion of fifty years ago — save for the crinoline — is their fashion to-day. With them colour, not style, is worshipped. But, for my part, I can see no difference between the worship of style and the worship of colour. Solomon would have called both vanity, when carried to such excess.

There is another kind of diarist — the variety which makes a note of any spirited expressions that are used in the pulpit. This type is also feminine. Having obtained a collection of sentences which they deem too vigorous for pulpit use, they send them along to the bishop. No one objects to a Church member complaining to the clergyman if there is any matter that the member dislikes. But it certainly comes as a surprise to a rector to find that some of his congregation, instead of approaching him, go quietly over his head to injure him in the eyes of his superiors.

Another type in my congregation I have classified under the heading of "Prompters." These are the good souls who know the Church services and ritual so thoroughly that the slightest mistake causes them exquisite suffering. So they sit far up the church in the pews which are near to the rector, and volunteer their assistance when the slip — for which they seem to have been watching — does eventually occur. And so I occasionally hear a loud whisper saying, " No, not Hymn 140, Hymn 130," or

"Please go slower, rector," or, "Please don't forget the benediction." I remember on one occasion that after I had pronounced the absolution, one imperious lady worshipper, who had forgotten, or not heard it, stood up in her pew and authoritatively commanded, " Please pronounce the absolution."

Such behaviour is, of course, brawling in church, and flagrantly illegal. Though there are members of a rural congregation who seem to be always too ready to take legal steps against their rector if he does not dovetail in with their ideas. I took care not to show openly how much I resented such interference on the part of women in my congregation. On this particular occasion I actually pronounced the absolution twice, so that my interrupter should not feel that she had missed any part of the service.

Yet another type is represented by the women who take charge of their husbands in church. I have seen them enter with a spouse, who seems to be decidedly frightened of his wife's frown. Some of the wives go further than frowning. They nudge their husbands, and sometimes kick them behind the shelter of a pew. When the service is over some of these women will spend as long as a quarter of an hour kneeling in silent prayer, while these husbands, holding her sable coat, pace up and down the aisle waiting. The devotions over, the patient husband helps his wife into her furs. She then takes charge again, and leads her husband out to the waiting car. Their religious observances are over for the week!

When I preached upon the practices of some of the ladies of fashion, I had a glimpse of yet another type. This kind, I think, can be classed as the literary variety. They bring their own literature with them into church. As soon as I start my sermon they produce a new novel with a gaudy cover — the latest effort of Marie Corelli or Elinor Glynn!

There is nothing surreptitious about their reading in church. They do not rest the book on their lap and make pretence that they are reading the Prayer-book or the Scriptures. Instead, they hold the novel high up before their face and turn over the leaves, careless of the rustling, which can be heard clearly all over the church.

Next come those with the offensive manners. We have at

Rusper a custom which should have been broken away from ages ago. When a house is let or sold, a pew in the village church is let or sold with it. The occupant of the house has the sole right to the use of this pew during church services. Some of these pew-owners come to a service perhaps once in six months, yet they expect to find their pew swept and garnished and vacant, ready for their exclusive use when they make their casual appearance.

It has often happened that the crowds that have come to Rusper, many of them drawn from outlying districts, have so filled the church that some of these neglected pews have had to be opened to provide the strangers with a seat in the House of God.

Some of the "pew-owners" have occasionally decided to attend church on one of these full days. Arriving late, they are horrified and indignant to find their long-neglected pew occupied, and so they call the churchwarden and the verger, and insist that the new-comers be turned out, and this has to be done. It is like a scene in the theatre or a circus. And I am powerless to interfere!

There are others whose behaviour in this church entitles them to be classed with those whose manners are offensive. Some German people who resided in the district used to come to church during the war. No one in my congregation could have hated the deeds of their countrymen more than I did. Yet there was no reason why these people should not attend the House of God, even if we were at war with their nation. Personally, I certainly had no intention of asking them to stay away.

Nevertheless, some of my congregation acted as though they believed it was my duty to decline them admittance. Some went further, and publicly insulted them in the House of God. I have seen professedly devout ladies worshipping in the church at Rusper, and at the same time making facial contortions at the Germans, who had also come in to worship. Some of these ladies even forgot their manners so far as to thrust out their tongues in the direction of the German pew.

Then there is the fussy type — the person who thinks the sermon too long, and says so by an assumed cough; the person who thinks the sermon is too short, and tells me so by look or word; the person who orders the verger or churchwarden to open the windows and the door, and the person in the next pew who immediately insists on their being shut again; the person who sends notes to the choirmaster and organist, and orders them to sing or play more reverently, or more slowly, or use different music.

There is also the type who concentrate not so much on what the rector says, as on what he does. This type is greatly concerned if he turns a couple of degrees beyond due east, or the same number of degrees less than due east during the recitation of the Creeds. This type of critic has objections to the way the rector wears his watch chain, and is much concerned that he should clasp his hands in a particular way when pronouncing the benediction. Should the rector by any chance put his hand in his cassock pocket, the action is immediately spotted by this type of worshipper, who soon acquaints him with what he terms his remissness in clerical etiquette.

One or two ladies specialise in footwear. They scrutinise my boots to see that they are properly blackened, and that the polish is of the radiance which they consider to be requisite. They do not forget the laces and the style of lacing, and, of course, the quality of the footwear. Should I, on a stormy evening, enter the church with a heavy pair of boots, instead of the dainty sanctuary shoes on which they insist, the incident becomes the gossip of the parish during the next twenty-four hours. By the end of the week this event has been handled with such imaginative hostility that I am being described as the parson who preaches in sporting-dress, in Wellington boots, and a light tweed suit.

Fortunately, with all these and many more strange types in my congregation, there is in Rusper a large sprinkling of devout and pious people who attend church to worship their Maker, not to criticise His people and His servant.

Chapter VII

MUSCULAR CHRISTIANITY

I have always believed in muscular Christianity. Rusper does not. It prefers the "I don't like London" type, as immortalised by the curate in "The Private Secretary."

When I was a young man in the Irish Constabulary, I was frequently mixed up in rough-and-tumbles. But for my skill with my fists, I might have gone under in those early days.

When I decided to give myself to the Church, I had no intention of preaching that the noble art of self-defence was a wicked pastime. I believe that the secret of the virility of the race is the ability of the average Britisher to take care of himself by using physical force.

I knew a clergyman whose interpretation of the text "If a man smite thee on the one cheek turn to him the other also," was that if the assailant took the second opportunity, it was up to the injured Christian to administer a sound thrashing.

One of my visitors during my first year in Rusper was a young woman who was in great distress because some vile gossip was being circulated by one of the men of the village about her.

"Have you a father?" I asked.

"No."

"Have you any brothers?"

"Oh, yes!"

"Well, go to your biggest brother, and tell him, with my compliments, that he is to go straight to this man who has been circulating these things about you. Tell him to demand an explanation and an apology, and," I added, "if he does not get it, tell him to punch his head!"

The girl looked at me with surprise. But she took my message.

I have had many experiences which have proved to me that muscular Christianity is oft-times a very good thing for the Church.

When I was a curate in a northern town, I had a very large Bible-class. As it was about the largest in the town, I suppose that I ought to have been content to rest on my oars. But I was not.

I took a stroll round the town and accosted some of the brawny young men, and invited them personally to come along to my class.

One of these was a young blacksmith — a fine, upstanding figure. I saw him at his forge with his sleeves rolled up displaying the most powerful equipment of muscles that I had seen since I left the police force.

"Good-morning, Tom!" I said. "Will you come along to my Bible-class to-morrow?"

Tom did not jump to accept.

"No, thanks!" he said. "You don't want fellows of my type there, and I prefer something a bit more vigorous for Sunday afternoons."

"Why, you don't work on Sundays, do you!"

"Oh, no!"

"Because if that is your trouble, I'll give you a hand to-day," I said.

Tom looked slightly incredulous.

"Have a try."

I took off my clerical coat and swung the hammer while he looked on.

"You'd do, sir, after a bit of practice," said he generously.

"But what about the Bible-class?" I persisted.

"Can't be done, sir! You see, every Sunday afternoon I get out on to the Heath with some of my pals, and we have a few rounds with the gloves. That's more in my line."

"Well, just you bring your pals and your gloves along to my Bible-class on Sunday afternoon, and when it's over you can have a few rounds in one of the sheds near by," I suggested.

"Do you mean that, sir?" said Tom, his eyes sparkling.

I said that I not only meant it, but I was prepared to put on the gloves myself with the best of them.

"Done!" exclaimed Tom. "We'll be along, and I'll box you myself."

Tom kept his word. We had a record attendance at the Bible-class, and when the lesson was finished, we all went off to a place near by where Tom and I had an encounter while all the rest of the class looked on.

I did not know until afterwards, that Tom the blacksmith was the champion of the town, or I might not have been quite so ready to take him on, as I had not boxed for a long time.

As I had my class watching, I felt that I must show all my old form if I was not to lose prestige with these lads.

Tom got home some very telling blows during the first few rounds. But in the fourth round he gave me an opening, and Tom was counted out.

Tom got up and shook hands readily enough, but he after-wards confessed to me it was the most unpleasant experience of his boxing life "to be knocked out by a curate!"

During my term at Rusper I have had one experience at least in which I found that practical experience with the gloves was very useful.

One day I bought a horse from two dealers. I expected to be taken in, as I know that this is the experience of everybody who buys a horse. But I was not prepared to fall in so deeply as I did over this precious pair.

When we put the animal into the stable, he started to kick the place to pieces. He kicked all the afternoon and well on into the night. He smashed the walls and anything that happened to be in range.

When he had battered that part of his stable within reach of his hind legs, he changed over and began again with his forelegs. He pawed the manger and smashed it; he broke the hay-rack, and kicked a hole in front of his nose big enough to thrust his head through. It would have been a good thing for me if he had made an opening big enough to escape. For it would have saved me much trouble, worry and expense.

The sequel to this unfortunate deal came a few weeks later. I was wandering down one of the lanes not far from Rusper when

I met these two precious dealers.

For five full minutes I talked to them upon their methods of business, and at the end of that little oration, both of them were in a state verging on apoplexy.

"If you were in any other garb, this would be your last speech!" one of them burst out.

That did it. I took off my coat and hat, and gave those two the soundest drubbing they had ever had.

Of the subsequent dealings of this precious pair I have no knowledge, but I am tolerably certain they waited a long time before they sold a bad-tempered horse to another clergyman.

CHAPTER VIII

WHEN THE NUNS GOSSIPED

During the early days of my five years at Rusper, I made an important discovery. I found that the gossiping mania which has affected and still affects a large percentage of the residents of Rusper is no new thing in the life of the village.

Seven centuries ago Rusper was notorious as a home of gossip. In those days there were no newspapers and magazines to make known to the whole country the great weakness from which this parish suffers. Yet even in those remote times the talking women of Rusper had attained to fame in towns and villages far beyond the parish borders.

There must be something in the soil or the air of this village which produces the finished gossiper. Perhaps some of my readers may be able to discover what it is from a brief description of the village and its history.

Rusper is set on a hill some 400 feet above sea level, commanding extensive views of the four counties of Surrey, Sussex, Hants, and Kent. The church occupies the highest point of eminence. The winds of God have played round its massive Norman towers for the past 800 years; the birds — those exquisite creatures of the Creator — have had their habitation in its towers for centuries past. In old times it was a Priory Church, and the mother church of many churches in the neighbourhood, including the beautiful parish church of the town of Horsham, on which it smiles down.

To Rusper's church was attached a monastery and nunnery — the priory in the east, and the nunnery in the south — each connected with the church by a subterranean passage.

Now, the first mention of Rusper as a gossiper's paradise was in those days when the monks and nuns were living in the village. In the ecclesiastical annals of Rusper there is written clearly for all to see that the nuns of Rusper did not obey the golden rule of silence. The charge of the Bishop of those days is still in print. It states that in the thirteenth century the Bishop of Chichester paid a special visit to Rusper to impose the vow of silence on the sisterhood.

But these definite instructions must have been mislaid before they reached the nuns of Rusper, or the holy women must have resented any interference with what may have been even in those days a recognised custom. Perhaps it was the garden produce, the water supply, the Rusper air, or some other equally compelling cause that was responsible for what followed. That I have not yet been able to discover.

Certain it is, however, that this vow of silence was flagrantly disobeyed, and that the nuns of the village indulged their practice of gossiping even as the residents of Rusper do to this day.

About a year after the vow had been imposed, the fame of the busy tongues of the Rusper sisterhood again reached the ears of the Bishop of Chichester, who this time found it necessary to enforce the vow of silence. Exactly how he enforced it I do not know. His methods are a lost secret. If the lost art could be discovered, I am convinced that it would be a very valuable find for Rusper.

It would be more valuable as far as this village, and perhaps many others, is concerned, than the discovery of the other lost art by which those exquisite blue colourings were obtained in the stained-glass windows of churches of the early Middle Ages.

The nunnery has disappeared from Rusper, but the whispering gallery has been perpetuated to this day. On the same ground where trod the whispering nuns, sweet flowers now grow. But amongst these flowers there has grown during my time the red bloom of scandal.

The far-off whispers of ancient days are buried. The scars and wounds of Nature are healed by the passage of time, but the breath of Nature cannot heal the wounds of the heart that is lacerated by the evil-tongue of the calumniator. The peach may restore its lost bloom; the violet its lost perfume; and sullied snow turn white in overnight, and leprosy be cleansed, but nought can cure the wounds that idle gossip can make in a rural parish.

Falsehoods, we are told, have no legs and cannot stand. But in Rusper they not only stand, but walk and run and never weary.

One morning during the first year of my ministry, I met a villager who warned me that there was a curse on the Rusper rectory.

"What is that!" I asked.

The villager hesitated, and then he said that every rector of the place for generations had illegally held a jewelled cross which was not his property. Until that was restored, he said, there would be a curse on every occupant of the rectory.

"Where is the cross?" I asked.

"You've got it, sir, I'm told," was the villager's retort.

"But I've never heard of such a thing as a jewelled cross in Rusper!" I exclaimed.

"It's in your house, sir."

"You'd better come along and show it to me," said I. "I'd like to have a look at it."

The villager shook his head and walked away, leaving me very puzzled.

I set to work to discover what was the foundation of this strange story. It appears that some years ago, in mid-Victorian days, the bodies of four nuns, including a prioress, were exhumed at the nunnery. In one hand of the prioress was a chalice; in the other hand, so the story runs, was a cross. As a matter of fact, no cross was ever discovered. Yet the story persists in the village that succeeding rectors, including myself, have possessed this cross.

I have been told that it is in a dark room at the end of a long passage in the rectory. I have heard it alleged that I have pawned it, redeemed it, and pawned it and redeemed it again. Nearly everyone but myself knows all about it. And until I restore it to its proper place, the curse of God will remain on the rector, his family, the church and parish.

The chalice is in safe keeping at the bank. It will be brought to the church for service on Easter Day. Though the jewelled cross, which exists only in the imagination of the village tittle-tattlers, is not at the rectory, there is, nevertheless, a cross in this old dwelling. Like the jewelled cross of tradition, it is invisible.

It is my own private cross made by cruel tongues; but it is a cross which I propose to bear until I have exposed and stamped out some of the gossiping and its attendant evils from the parishes of England.

CHAPTER IX

MEN IN MY PARISH

Many of the men in my parish are women! By this I mean that they have the gossiping instinct developed to as high a degree as have some of their mothers, sisters, wives, and daughters.

Until I came to Rusper, I believed that men in the mass, were more charitable and took a wider view of things than many women. I still believe that this is true with the bulk of the male population of the country.

It is not true in Rusper. The tongue of the male gossiper is as uncharitable and ready to utter a falsehood as that of any scorned woman.

The supreme passion of my work in the church, since my ordination twenty-one years ago, has been to labour among men. I have always been a man's man and minister. I hope that I always shall be.

My six years in the Royal Irish Constabulary, to which I have already referred, brought me into touch with the finest body of men in the world. As a musketry instructor, I trained thousands of them in Phoenix Park.

I have always observed with the greatest regret that the male element is usually a minority in our churches. It struck me forcibly when I was first ordained, and I determined that I would preach the religion that would appeal to the men.

From my first sermon I have always preferred to address men, and I have almost invariably succeeded in filling my churches with men.

In North London I enjoyed the luxury of preaching to 1,000 or more men on Sunday afternoons — and those were days in a sultry August, when half the men of the parish were on holiday, and the other half might have been excused for preferring a smoke and a walk in the park.

I knew that I could draw these Londoners to church on a Sunday afternoon, but when I was offered, by Sir John Jackson, the chaplaincy of the Keyham Dockyard at Devonport, my opinions marked time. Could I draw the artisan and the Navy? I asked myself. Experience proved that I was able to draw the artisan and the sailor in great crowds to the mission churches there, and on Sundays (to the number of 2,000) to the Public Hall.

I had a great grasp of the psychology of the London man and of the man of the big provincial towns; I did not realise until I came to Rusper how much the rustic and the village-dweller differed from these types.

I soon had occasion to remember the warning I received from a college professor during my college days. His words burned in my brain. His father, he told me, was a country rector in Sussex, and he had said that work in a Sussex village would make an atheist of any clergyman in seven years.

I have overcome, but can now understand what lay beneath that latter remark. Faith that has a solid foundation is not undermined by the unpleasant manners, methods, and morals of a Sussex village.

Soon after I arrived I had occasion to turn up Carlyle. Previously I had not been able to subscribe to the view that I then read. But I have had ample reason to do so since.

Writing to his wife, Carlyle tells her that the "babbling, inconclusive nature of the rustic population here, if you have anything to do with them, is altogether beyond a jest. I positively feel it immoral and disquieting. I avoid all company whatever with them, except the few poor, greedy-minded, very stupid rustics, who have some affairs with me, which I struggle always to cut short. I am willing to exchange the country, with all its beauty, for the smoke, turmoil, and dirt of Chelsea."

This was Carlyle's description of his life in rural England

nearly a century ago. If that great master could come back to England and spend a few weeks at Rusper, he would have no reason for altering his writings by as much as a comma.

And not Rusper only, but numerous villages all over the country could be similarly described, if my colleagues of the cloth had the courage to speak publicly of their experiences, as hundreds have done verbally and by letter to me.

Only this week I met a brother clergyman, to whom I mentioned these articles. He congratulated me on my courage, and lamented that he dared not risk the outcry and social ostracism which might follow, if he ventured to do the same.

If I divide the men of Rusper into classes or groups, my readers must not forget that the parish is still semi-feudal. The security of the farmer and labourer is dependent upon the good-will of his feudal lord. The feudal lord of the eleventh century, it is true, has gone. His place is taken, not by one, but by many who have money and no pedigree. They establish themselves in the fond hope that they will be regarded as squires and squiresses.

Amongst the farmers and their labourers, and the old aristocracy here I have many staunch friends. Much of the trouble and the gossip in the village can be traced to the new-rich and their relatives.

With people of this new class a rector stands much on the level of a butler or head housemaid, though he may not be so well paid as the chauffeur. I really believe they expect him to use the tradesmen's entrance!

The men of the village, whether traders, or labourers, farmers or new-rich, carry on the great gossiping craze daily. Gossip may go from house to house, wrapped in a case of whisky, packed in a packet of tea, or contained in the ration of sugar. It is taken to the doctor, the baker, the candlestick maker, and undertaker.

Some of the houses in Rusper will open their doors wide to any man that brings it. The tradesman with his wares, or the decorator with his whitewash-brush, the labourer with his hay-fork — all will be welcomed, if they will only come and tell some new tale of their neighbour's mode of life.

Lord Macaulay, in one of his essays, describes the Bengalee thus:—

"What the horns are to the buffalo, what beauty is to the woman, what the sting is to the bee, deceit is to the Bengalee."

What deceit is to the Bengalee, scandal is to sixty per cent, of the men of Rusper!

CHAPTER X

WOMEN OF THE VILLAGE

There are no Helens of Troy in Rusper. There are no women, who, like Hero, the priestess of Venus, could inspire the modern Leanders of Sussex to swim the Hellespont nightly for the sake of a few brief moments of sweet converse.

Beauty does not bloom here! Beauty, I know, is not an accomplishment. It is one of those gifts to humanity which Nature bestows with a sparing hand.

But I have seen beauty shining through plain and even ugly faces — beauty that is more than skin-deep; beauty which is produced by a noble soul, daily occupied with high thoughts and kindly deeds.

There are some of these noble and beautiful women among the female population of this and every village in England. They are the leaven which I hope will one day leaven the whole fraternity of village women.

Other women there are, who denied beauty of face or form, make themselves still more repellent by their thoughts, their words and deeds. Long hours spent in idle and venomous gossip seems to leave a mark on their plain and vacant faces. I can tell a gossiper and scandalmonger by a glance, even as a doctor can frequently recognise the disease from which a person is suffering by looking into the eyes or at the tongue.

Love of scandal is written plainly on the faces of these women everywhere. If any modern artist is in need of a model to express the voice of the calumniator in any great work that he is undertaking, he could not do better than come to Rusper and stroll down our village street. He would soon procure such a perfect model of a female slanderer that the fame of his picture would be assured.

When first I came to Rusper, the women of the village reminded me of the statue of Buddha. Travellers in India observe a statue of Buddha at the entrance to most of the temples, and the most striking thing about these statues is the length of Buddha's tongue, which is coiled round his neck. The tongues of the women of Rusper do not reach round their necks, but they stretch from door to door and even from parish to parish.

If I had courteously waited and listened, instead of shortening their tales with a curt criticism, I should have spent many weary hours listening to these long and active female tongues.

This is the third time that I have penned an article on women.

My first attempt was an essay at a competitive examination when I was in the last years of my teens. Out of these subjects I chose the visit of Queen Alexandra to Egypt and the Nile. That essay I elaborated and sent to the editor of an Irish paper. He sent me the first money that I had ever earned — ten pounds. I accepted that sum with compliments and thinks. Those were the days when I had more manners than money.

I remember in that essay describing the princess (as she then was), as a fairy goddess of immaculate purity and beauty, as bright as the sun, glorious as the moon, and lustrous as the stars.

In those days I so regarded all women. I did not dream that one day I should turn my crude pen to write disdainfully, and perhaps even despairingly, of any daughter of Eve.

When the fabled king sent for Hercules to cleanse the Aegean Stables, he accomplished by stealth what a thousand men could not do by strength. He diverted the waters of a mighty stream, and so cleansed the stables.

A man with more strength and stealth than ever the thews and sinews of Hercules could boast, is needed to frustrate the fortified idolatries of slander in the villages of "silly" Sussex, Surrey, and most of the other counties of modern England.

Many painful sensations have I felt as I have walked up and

down the Via Dolorosa of the village of Rusper during the last five years.

Cicero galled many of his contemporaries when he said, "I wish the Forum were paved with sharp shells," as he watched the idle quidnunes lounging about.

I should like to transfer some of the sharp stones from the Eastern plains to scorch the feet of those women who go about whispering the ill-conceived prejudices of feeble minds.

In our villages the women move in little cliques. A member of one clique will not willingly be seen talking to a member of another clique. And if she is so caught, she has lost much caste.

Some of these cliques have a specially appointed liaison-officer, who goes between them and reveals to one clique what is being said of their members by those in the other clique.

Others, who count themselves among the great, the elite, and the gods of the village, employ a kind of woman scout — a member of a slightly lower grade — to be their trumpeter, and to sing their praises. I have often remarked upon the indolence of some of our women. They would have voted against the Day-light Saving Act on principle. That extra hour out of bed in the morning brings them no joy.

They rise about eight or nine o'clock, and come downstairs for their breakfast, which has, in some cases, been prepared for them by their husbands. Then they go back to bed again for several hours.

Most of their time is spent in one another's houses, except on washing-days, when they are mostly in the garden. So many hours do they spend gossiping over the garden-fence that their clothes are dry and ready to be taken in by the time their tongues are tired and the secret history of all their neighbours has been brought up-to-date.

Seventy-five per cent, of the women of Rusper are absolutely devoid of a sense of humour. They cannot see a joke even if you explain it to them for half an hour.

I think this unhappy state of theirs is largely occasioned by the fact that we are so many miles away from the towns and the railway. The people here marry and inter-marry, so that every household is related to almost every other household in the village. Almost all are cousins, aunts, and uncles, once, twice, or thrice removed, and relationship is claimed and fostered.

Some of the women of our villages divide the whole population into two classes — those who have worked with their hands, or have been in business, and those who have never soiled their hands, and who know nothing of business. And the former, naturally, in their own opinion, are miles above the latter. The Jews have no use for the Samaritans.

Yet members of this "non-manual and non-business" class may themselves have inherited their money from people who have been bakers or farmers, grocers or shoeblacks, sweeps or pill-makers.

They do not seem to realise the fundamental truth that each person who is doing his duty to his country sells his labour to others; it may be the labour of his brain, or of his hands. Yet they will receive no one into their clique who can be proved either to have bought or sold. Some of the members of these exclusive cliques will take great pains to inquire into the antecedents of newcomers to the village, so that they may not by mistake welcome one who is not of their noble ilk.

These super-superior persons imagine themselves the salt of the village. Poor blind creatures! If they could but see their contemptible conduct as it really is; could they but test it by the real standards of worth and usefulness to their fellow-creatures, how small and insignificant they would feel!

They would want to hide themselves in the kitchen of the grimy-handed peasant saint, whose work, in the eyes of God and sane-thinking men, elevates him to a pinnacle beyond the vision of such small-minded and purse-proud female Pharisees.

To my thinking the most offensive aspect of these superior women is their assumption of deep piety. Though they could not think of speaking on equal terms with one who has bought or sold a business, they consider, nevertheless, that they are among God's specially chosen. Yet Christ selected his followers from the poor and lowly.

This state of affairs I feel sure has an evil effect upon the people. They want an infusion of new blood. As in other parts of England, there is here a preponderance of females over males. It would be a great thing for the life of the village if some of the young men of Horsham, Guildford, Brighton, or Three Bridges, when seeking their wives, would come over to Rusper, and so prevent this inter-marrying of relations which is so common here.

On the other hand, I would counsel some of the lads of the village to go farther afield to seek their wives. Then perhaps we should see a great change come over the village. Humour might reappear and gossip might pass its present zenith, and decline.

I once told a group of local women the story of the Irishman who informed a friend that he was afraid that his wife had contracted lockjaw, as she had not spoken to him for a week.

"You always were a lucky fellow," was his friend's retort. "If it's catching I'll ask my wife to call round and see her to-day."

This story was lost on the women of my parish.

CHAPTER XI

PARISH PARASITES

Some clergymen make a reputation as good beggars. In Rusper, the clergyman, not the parishioners, is regarded as fair game by people who are financially embarrassed.

I came to Rusper with £6,000 in my pocket. At the end of five years I am worth about sixpence. Much of this £6,000, it is true, had to be squandered on legal expenses to meet the frivolous charges which any Church member can, and some Church members did, bring against me.

Not all this sum, however, was swallowed by the courts.

The question that was first asked about me after my advent in Rusper was "Has he any money? What is he worth?"

Whence came the answer, I cannot say. Certainly not from me, my household, or my bank. Yet Rusper knew almost to a penny how much I was worth within a week of my arrival.

The begging letters began to arrive early, and one of these opened with the following amazing sentence: "Since you are a comparatively rich man, with over £6,000, and are known to be of a generous disposition, I beg to ask you to help my family..."

I put the letter down on the table and breathed hard.

"The good folk of Rusper seem to know all about my business already," I remarked to my wife.

I felt inclined to write back to this worthy soul and ask him if he would be good enough to keep a daily diary for me, since he was so well acquainted with my private affairs.

Other good people began a practice which was none the less interesting, although it added to the duties of my servant, who was frequently disturbed by the ringing of the front door bell. The callers were invariably persons of the tramp and impecunious class. Their visits became so frequent that one day I said to a parishioner:

"The county must be full of beggars, if I may judge by the number of persons soliciting alms at the rectory door."

"Well, sir," rejoined the parishioner, "everybody knows as you are a wealthy man, so that we always tells people of that type to come down and see you. They used to do the same with your predecessors."

The villager had opened my eyes still further. I was to be regarded as the local relieving-officer, not only to those poor beggars who were in difficulties, but to others better off than myself, who were shirking their own moral obligations by passing these unfortunates on to me.

I made a mental note of this practice for reference in a future sermon. But the persons who were ready to share with me my few thousands continued to grow in number.

One morning a well-dressed lady who did not live far beyond the boundaries of the parish, and who had occasionally come to hear my sermons, presented herself at my door. She stated that her husband was financially embarrassed, and unless he could produce £50 by that afternoon the consequences for the pair would be dire indeed. Would I lend the sum for a few days?

The story was undoubtedly true, and so I wrote out the cheque for £50. The cheque was cashed in due course. I did not press for payment. The time came, however, when I did express a readiness to receive the return of the loan at the convenience of the borrower.

At length the borrower decided to pay in an unusual way. I was offered a horse which was a good hunter, I accepted the offer, and asked a jockey to take him out for a ride. My luck with this horse was even worse than I experienced with the animal I bought from the two dealers.

The jockey rode this horse to a neighbouring town, where my new mount distinguished himself by jumping through a very tempting plate-glass window.

The injuries sustained by the unfortunate jockey were rather serious, and the cost of maintaining him and meeting doctor's bills during the next seven weeks was £70.

Then I had a claim from the shopkeepers for the damage to their shattered window. This was a modest little sum of about £10. As for the horse, the poor animal had been so badly cut about that it had to be destroyed. I did save the cost of this tragedy by shooting him myself !

I think that everyone will agree with me when I say that I did not come off well over this loan. I had already parted with £50, and had to spend another £80 — £130 in all — with nothing in hand at the end.

Another needy person came one day to borrow £90. He explained that my predecessor had occasionally been very kind to him when in difficulties, and had always found him an honest man. I agreed to lend him the money, but was again repaid in kind, and lost more than half of my money.

My small fortune was visibly dropping before my legal expenses began.

I record it with sorrow that the average villager does not ask the social standing of a newcomer — whether he has blue blood or porridge in his veins The one and only question he asks is: Has he money?

The usual comment is: "If he ain't got no money he be no good to me."

When the villagers realised that my little fortune of £6,000 was not likely to go far, I received a candid communication to the effect that I was not much good now unless I could get some more money.

This opinion was shared by some of the more affluent pillars of the church. Once I invited the ladies of the church to come and join in a spring-cleaning. I was approached by one pillar of the church, who said that this request was an insult to the ladies; he added that my predecessors used to pay charwomen to do the cleaning. My innovation meant that I was taking away the living of the local charwomen.

"Why did you come here when you had not a private income of £1,000 a year?" demanded another. "All your predecessors," he continued, "were fools, but they had money."

"I told him that I was here to preach the Word of God not to administer charity; to give of the Water of Life; but now realised that I was expected to be the local banker, moneylender, and philanthropist rolled into one.

CHAPTER XII

VILLAGE TALENT

A mong the society of the parish there is a section who wish to figure as patrons of the poor. From time to time they discover new methods of improving the lot of the villagers. Of course they do not consult the rector or his wife, as they want to receive all the glory and kudos which may accrue from these innovations

Without spending the necessary time in thinking out their schemes, they start village arts and crafts, small classes for cooking, sewing meetings for Susie to make shirts or skirts, meetings for votes for girls, Shakespeare classes for farmers' boys, seances for widows and orphans, knitting lessons for wounded soldiers, singing classes for the future musical "stars" of the village, Futurist art classes for carters' mates, or natural history lessons for village butchers.

Great movements such as these are always either beginning or expiring.

One woman with much time on her hands reads in a magazine that some such innovation has been a great success in Timbuctoo or Tokyo, and she immediately decides that this is exactly what the unenlightened folk of our villages need to interest and illuminate their dull, heavy minds. In a flash it is sprung upon them.

Villagers are always ready to welcome some new thing, and since Mrs. So-and-So is paying for the hall, or giving a free tea at the first performance, they roll up. But, as can be well appreciated, they soon tire of Mrs. So-and-So's new fad. And

Mrs. So-and-So wonders why, forgetting that whereas she has ample time on her hands to think out this and many other betterment schemes, the poor folk have been working for a master from 6 a.m. until the evening, and then have to resume work for themselves in their own garden during the few hours that are still left of daylight.

Occasionally I have mooted some scheme which, in my own opinion, would prove a source of mental benefit to some of the villagers, and have been amazed to find that while I was carefully developing the plans some of the busybodies of the locality have stepped in before me. The first intimation that I have received of their intention has been a gaudily-printed bill announcing my scheme and summoning the villagers to the parish hall for the "grand" inaugural meeting fixed for that evening.

To have the ground cut from under his feet is not a pleasant experience for the village rector, and these busybodies who want to be somebodies ought not to be offended if the rector occasionally expresses himself vigorously upon their actions. Yet the men and women of Rusper need instruction in the arts. They lack accomplishments. They have money, but, as a rule, little talent.

If I had occasion to seek a woman who could play or sing, I almost invariably sought in vain. And yet if only one per cent, of the time they have expended in gossip during the past five years that I have been here had been devoted to the development of latent talent, our men and women would doubtless be as accomplished as those in any town or city parish.

The piano-player and the gramophone, which are learnt without tears and toil, are far too popular for the development of local talent.

Once I had occasion to call for a song from some lady member of an audience at a village festival. For a long time I could get no response. I was new to the village in those days, and innocently assumed that the women suffered from the shyness for which they are famed. So I suggested to one lady who sat near the platform in one of the expensive seats that she might like to oblige. She came forward, modestly protesting that she could not sing, as every amateur singer invariably does. In her case, however, I had no reason to doubt her afterwards.

As I sat and listened to her vocal efforts, that satirical couplet from Coleridge, "On a Bad Singer," came into my mind:

"Swans sing before they die. 'Twere no bad thing
Did certain persons die before they sing."

While I sympathised with this good lady's willingness to oblige us, I felt constrained to say to her afterwards: "The next time that you tell me you cannot sing I'll believe you."

I know that I shall be severely criticised for daring to write on village arts. None who has ever written on the thorny subject of the arts has yet escaped attack. As Kipling says:

"When the flush of a new-born sun fell first on Eden's
green and gold,
Our father Adam sat under a tree and scratched
with a stick in the mould;
And the first rude sketch that the world had seen
was joy to his mighty heart,
Till the Devil whispered behind the leaves: 'It's
pretty, but is it art?' "

Despite Kipling, it would be a great thing if we could change the men and women of the village so that instead of gossiping about their neighbours they could speak in an enlightened way upon our artistic accomplishments. Art criticism and gossip are as sunshine and storm.

Some of the society of the parish consider that they can teach the cottagers by entering their homes and making suggestions. Many of these I have dubbed "the economic women."

As I go round, I hear of their visits to the struggling poor, and the uncomplimentary things that the villagers say of them. They roll up to the doors of the little cottages in beautiful motor-cars, and clothed in costly furs, beseech the housewives to be economical, as only by thrift can the country be saved from the great financial crisis through which it is passing.

They talk glibly of thrift to women who have spent their lives trying to feed and clothe their husbands and children on a wage of about twenty-five shillings a week. They tell them how to plant their gardens, and how to boil the potatoes in their jackets, so as to avoid waste in the peeling, and so on.

Having delivered themselves in this wise for half an hour, they go back to their motor-car and drive home to their sumptuous dinner, comprising out-of-season fruits at prices per pound more than the weekly income of the household they have visited.

One of the cottagers expressed her opinion of these visitors to me in very plain language:

"They talk of economy and extravagance." she said. "Why, I never knew what extravagance was until I heard from one of their servants what these economical ladies like for dinner!"

Her remark reminded me of the visit of a very famous preacher to an out-of-the-way Irish town. After preaching a powerful sermon on sin, he was approached by a poor woman in the congregation, who had received much spiritual help from his discourse. Thinking to show her appreciation, she said to him:

"Father, we never knew the manin' of sin until you came here!"

If some of these "economical ladies" changed their tactics and gave free music lessons to the daughter of the house, or spent an hour or two in giving practical instruction in art needlework or painting, they might have made a better impression, and have been welcomed next time.

CHAPTER XIII

MY FARMING ADVENTURES

There are many things prohibited to a clergyman by the canons of the Church of England. He must not:

Wear red socks.
Wear grey clothes.
Frequent public-houses.
Spend his time idly playing cards or throwing dice.
Farm more than eighty acres without the consent of the Bishop.

I love farming, and when the war suspended some of the canons of the Church, the way was opened for me to take up farming in real earnest.

The clergy were invited to go out and work on farms and in factories under the National Service scheme. Many of the clergy responded to the invitations, and became producers as well as preachers.

Previous to the war I had farmed the statutory number of acres, and, of course, some local busybody wrote to the Bishop and alleged that I was breaking the Church canons through being a farmer. Oh, these local busybodies! When will they learn to mind their own business?

When war was declared, I wrote to the War Office and offered my services in any capacity in which they chose to use me. I specially mentioned that I had had experience as a drill-instructor, and also farmed eighty acres of land.

I had always understood that writing to the War Office was

like sending a message to Mars — no satisfaction and usually no answer was ever received.

I have no complaint to make of my experience of the War Office. I had an early reply, which stated that I could best serve my country by taking up the chaplaincy at the military camp at Horsham, and by taking up farm work in the parish. I accepted both suggestions.

A farm of 400 acres had just become vacant, and was offered to me. This farm I worked successfully for three years, and carried on my parish duties at the same time. I worked early and late, in all seasons and in all weathers.

During 1916 1 established a record for hard work. With only three men and two horses I cut 100 acres of hay, thirty acres of harvest, and milked twenty-five cows twice daily.

During the week-days the work was strenuous, in very truth! But Sundays! The recollection of those times makes me look round for a chair.

On Sunday mornings I arose at four o'clock. 1 walked across to the farm and helped to tie up the cows in the stalls. I then milked twelve cows and helped to carry the milk to the carts.

Then I turned my attentions to the calves and fed half a dozen of them. The poultry next demanded my care. After these had been fed, I hurried back to the rectory, took my bath, and dressed for Holy Communion.

At eight-thirty a.m. I swallowed my breakfast in ten minutes, as I had to hurry off to Roffey Camp, five miles away, to preach to the soldiers at their nine-thirty church parade.

This service lasted three-quarters of an hour, which left me barely time to get back to Rusper Church for morning service at eleven.

As I had no curate, I conducted the service right through, preached for half an hour, and often celebrated Holy Communion afterwards.

From one until three I had lunch and a brief respite, and then I was back again in the school conducting the children's Sunday afternoon service. I played the music, taught the scholars, and gave an address as well.

This service was over at three forty-five, and I would then rush off to the byres again to repeat the work that I had been doing in the early morning — now twelve hours away. Having again milked the cows, and fed the calves and poultry, I returned to the rectory and prepared myself for Evensong at six-thirty.

Again I took the whole of the service, and it was eight o'clock before my labours for these arduous Sundays of sixteen hours were over.

But I enjoyed my life. I felt that I was doing my bit. As was to be expected, my efforts aroused more criticism than appreciation. Some thought and said that it was unseemly that a rector should rush through Sunday at this headlong speed. Others suggested that I was on the make, and was unfairly competing with legitimate farmers.

Unfair competition, indeed, when I was carrying out the wishes of the War Office, and trying to do my humble share to alleviate the food crisis through which we were passing on account of the German submarine campaign of frightfulness.

After I had been doing my bit in this strenuous fashion for a year or two I felt that I had earned a fortnight's holiday. So I resolved to look round for a *locum tenens*. But all the local clergy had their own Church duties to carry out.

As there are nearly 20,000 ordained clergymen in the Church of England, I thought that it ought not to be difficult to obtain a little help from some of my less hard-worked brother clergy resident in other parts of the country. I decided to advertise for assistance.

As I was drafting the advertisement it occurred to me that I ought to state clearly what were some of the duties of the office. So I drafted my advertisement on these lines:

Locum tenens wanted. Six guineas weekly offered. In addition to conducting ordinary Church services, he will be required to milk twelve cows and feed the poultry, both morning and after-noon. He will also have to preach at a soldiers' church parade at a camp five miles away.

The advertisement duly appeared, and I waited for the applicants' letters to arrive. But I waited in vain; there were no applicants.

By their silence my brother clergymen showed what they

thought of my life at Rusper. And I was forced to carry on without my holiday.

CHAPTER XIV

POACHERS ON MY FARM

The clothes that I wore on my farm, as was only to be expected, gave great offence. Those parishioners who have a burning passion for the melancholy black uniform standardised for clergymen were greatly hurt by the spectacle of their rector in the garb of "Varmer Giles."

There were some, however, whose attitude was different. "You seem to be more like one of us now!" said one of the local farmers, when he first met me in my land uniform. Another intimate friend called to me over the hedge, and recited this stanza from Hood's "The Surplice Question":

> "For me, I neither know nor care
> Whether a parson ought to wear
> A black dress or a white dress;
> Filled with a trouble of my own —
> A wife who preaches in her gown,
> And lectures in her nightdress!"

I called back to him, and expressed the hope that the verse he quoted did not really present his domestic situation. Whereat he laughed, and retorted that there were many husbands in this and most villages who could say these lines and mean each word.

Yet I made it a practice never to go out of the vestry without wearing my clerical collar. On my farm, on my holidays, wherever I have gone since I was ordained, I have always worn this clerical collar, so that all who saw me should have no doubts about my profession.

I have always been, and still am, as proud of my calling as the general is of the Army, the admiral of the Navy, the doctor of the medical profession — yes, and the Salvation Army lass of her noble order and her picturesque bonnet and most serviceable uniform.

Some of the clergy, I have heard occasionally change into mufti, and move about without conveying any indication of the office they hold. I can understand the feelings of a man who wants to reform the clerical uniform, but I cannot understand the attitude of a minister of the Church of England who wishes to hide his calling — the noblest calling of all!

As Bacon says in his Preface to the Law Tracts: "I hold every man a debtor to his profession; from the which, as men, of course, do seek to receive countenance and profit, so ought they of duty to endeavour themselves, by ways of amends, to be a help and ornament thereunto."

Which reminds me of an incident at the theological college where I was trained. Our Principal had a great objection to smoking by the students. There was a very emphatic regulation posted up throughout the college prohibiting smoking in any room. One day, as the Principal passed down the corridor outside my door, he looked into my room and asked: "Are you smoking, Synnott?" I was not.

"Someone is!" he declared, and sniffed all round the room. I, too, thought I could smell smoke.

"It must be in the next room, then," said the keen-nosed Principal. He burst into the next room, and there found a young student, a dour Scot, lying on his back, smoking up the chimney.

"What! Smoking!" exclaimed the Principal. "Don't you know it's contrary to regulations to smoke in your room?"

"Yes, sir," drily retorted the young Scot. "That's why I'm smoking up the chimney — there are no regulations against that!"

The Principal with difficulty repressed a smile. Soon afterwards he amended the smoking regulation, and worded it so carefully that not even an embryonic K.C. could find in it an excuse for a single puff within one hundred yards of the college.

Before I came to Rusper I rented a piece of ground at Worthing, and there had a little trouble with one good soul because of the noise made by the buglers of my Church Lads' Brigade, who came to practise on it. Another lady was intensely annoyed because some of the cocks crowed too loudly at dawn.

It seems that people will tolerate most things from an ordinary citizen or villager, but when a clergyman takes anything in hand he is looked at through different and more powerful spectacles.

There were plenty of noisy poultry in other parts of the town, yet my poultry, because they were owned by a clergyman, I suppose, were expected to be of a higher order. Some people seem to think that a clergyman's cockerels should produce the soothing notes of a cathedral organ!

While some objected to my taking a farm in the neighbourhood of Rusper, others saw in this proceeding a source of pleasure or profit to themselves. One or two of my more intimate friends came to me and asked if I wanted any help in keeping down the rabbits.

As rabbits had then become very scarce — that was before the control prices were fixed — and were saleable at from five shillings to ten shillings each, there was not a very grave danger of my few fields being overrun with them.

I gave permission to shoot to several of these friends. Many others of the neighbourhood did not trouble to ask permission. They took French leave — in season and out of season. The easygoing rector and his rabbits were fair game to them!

As I used to walk across my fields I would frequently discover little copper-wire nooses set in the rabbit-runs by some of my own or neighbouring parishioners. Others boldly brought their guns.

It was not lost upon the local poachers that the best time to shoot my rabbits was when I was conducting a service. Then the risk of being caught was small.

Sometimes, when I noticed that my morning congregation was smaller than usual, and that some well-known faces were missing, I could not help thinking that I knew where they had gone. They were busy elsewhere — on my farm, shooting my rabbits!

One of these local poachers, greatly daring, came to my house one morning and asked for the loan of my gun. He stated that he was being greatly troubled with rats, and proposed to undertake a great rat-hunt at his house that afternoon. I lent him my gun readily enough, suspecting nothing.

My surprise was great — and, I'm afraid, my indignation greater —when, late that evening, I took an unwonted stroll round my fields, and found the man who had borrowed my gun using it on the rabbits on my own farm!

"So this is how you shoot your rats, is it?" I asked.

The man looked very sheepish.

"I think I'll take that gun back now!" I said, and I relieved him of his borrowed weapon.

This incident was one of the choicest I experienced as a farmer. It reminded me of the old song, in which the singer is invited to play football with a borrowed silk hat. He jumps, and kicks, and kicks again, but doesn't know till afterwards that the hat was his own.

This incident is typical of the views that are held locally by a large percentage of the population; they consider that they have a right to anything that grows in the fields, and do not stop to think of the rights of the man who has to extract from those fields the money wherewith to pay the rent of his holding.

If I am told that the disciples plucked the ears of corn as they walked with their Lord by the cornfields, I answer readily that there is a great difference in the pulling of a few ears of corn to satisfy momentary hunger and the shooting — with his own gun — of a clergyman's rabbits for the purpose of making money As Lowell says:

> "Why law and order, honour, civil right,
> Ef they ain't worth, what is worth a fight?
> · · · · · · · · · · · ·
>
> The plough, the axe, the mill,
> All kinds o' labour, and kinds of skill,
> Would be a rabbit in a wild-cat's claw
> Ef 'tweren't for that slow crittur, 'stablished law."

I never sought the aid of the law to protect my farm from local poachers, although I had many incitements to do so.

Chapter XV

TAXES AND LOSSES

One disturbing experience of my farming days is still very prominent in my memory. It concerns yet another horse!

I had bought two big, heavy draft animals, over seventeen hands high, for the hard work on the stiff clay-soil of my farm.

My luck with horses, I fear, will become a byword. Not long after this new purchase one of these great Clydesdales was found drowned in a big pond on my farm. It had been driven into the deep water by some rowdies, not from my own, I am glad to say, but from an adjoining parish. The death of this unfortunate animal meant to me a loss of about £80.

This was not the only loss through drowning of a valued animal that I sustained as a farmer. On another occasion a valuable cow fell into the deep water of another pond, and was dead before it could be pulled out.

There were more troubles than with the drowned horse to follow the death of this cow. I was informed of my loss by one of the sidesmen. At this time there was snow, and the ground was hard-frozen — conditions in which a dead cow would keep for weeks.

Now it was brought to the knowledge of myself — the amateur farmer — that this cow must be buried forthwith, to comply with certain statutory regulations, which vary not, whether the weather is tropical or Arctic. My informants were two police-officers, who, passing my field, had observed my poor dead cow frozen stiff on the bank of the pond from which she had just been dragged.

I was informed that I had only a few hours left to get this carcass underground. I was busy, and assistance was difficult to get in those war days when everyone was short of labour. And so we were a few hours late in getting this poor old cow safely interned under the snow.

The inevitable followed! A blue paper, left by a man in blue, informed me that I must call at the Dorking Police-court to answer a charge of having broken the law by not burying this frozen cow in the statutory time. I was too busy to attend the court, but I learned subsequently that the grave Justice of the Peace for the town of Dorking had decided to console me for the loss of my cow by fining me one pound!

Time went on, and I had forgotten this precious fine. Winter had turned into spring, and summer was on us before it was again brought forcibly to my mind. I was busy in the field, gathering in the hay harvest, when two policemen climbed over the gate and walked towards me.

"Are you the Rector of Rusper?" they asked.

"Yes," I admitted, wondering at the same time why the police wanted to see me.

"We have a demand for the payment of a fine of one pound, and we have instructions not to return until it has been paid."

"Is it necessary for two strong men like you to be sent on such an errand when the Army is crying out for men to fight?" I asked. I'm afraid that remark got home.

"That's our instructions," was the answer.

I told them it looked very much as though they were out for a holiday. It was one of the most extraordinary things that has happened in my life — being waited on by two police-officers for a paltry pound.

"Have you nothing better to do in Dorking?" I asked them, and they did not answer. "Well, since you are here, and not very busy, perhaps you will give me a hand at haymaking? My farm," I explained, "like many other British farms and undertakings, just now badly needs a little assistance."

The police-officers did not fall in with my suggestion. It was the pound fine, not a job at haymaking, that they wanted.

As I was not in the habit of taking pound-notes into the hay-field, I informed them that they must wait until my work was done, and they could get it after I had been home to the rectory for it. And those two representatives of the law waited on through the day until my work was finished. But they got their "pound of my old cow's flesh!"

One other experience of the ways of rural authorities comes to my mind. I had spent a lot of money on various urgent needs, and was expecting a long over-due cheque, when one morning the income tax officer called upon me and suddenly demanded my income tax.

"You might have said that you were calling!" I protested, as I saw the collector in his trap at my door.

It appeared that this method of collection is a custom in the rural districts.

"Well, how much do you want?" I queried.

"A hundred and eighty-four pounds," was his answer.

"Can't be done!" I retorted.

The tax-collector hesitated.

"Well, I'll take half!" he volunteered at length.

I gave him half, and then I reminded him of the Irish priest who was famed for his fine library. One day one of his parishioners came and asked to borrow one of his books. The answer was that he could read it on condition that he stayed in the library.

Next day the priest was in need of a garden-roller, and he called upon his visitor of the previous evening, and asked for the loan of his.

"You can borrow my roller on condition that you only roll it up and down on my garden lawn!" was the, perhaps, not unnatural answer.

The tax-gatherer smiled, but when I told him that he would have to remain at the rectory until I had earned the other half, he declared that he was content, and drove away.

Southey has a very telling stanza about taxation in his poem, "The Devil's Walk":

> "Satan gave thereat his tail
> A twirl of admiration;
> For he thought of his daughter, War,
> And her suckling babe, Taxation."

Though tax-gatherers are very thorough and determined; though they sometimes come and dump their representatives into village houses and tell them to wait until the overdue taxes are paid, I would prefer to have a parish made up of tax-gatherers to a parish in which the venomous tongue causes more suffering than poverty or disease.

Chapter XVI

WHERE SLANDERS ARE HATCHED

Every village has, or should have, its local hall, its assembly rooms, its institute, its pavilion, its settlement, or its forum.

In some villages we find good-hearted men and women of wealth and leisure building and endowing an institution, which serves as a reading-room, a concert-hall, and a political platform.

I have entered some of these institutions and observed that they are gems of light and warmth, of learning and music, are conducted on model lines, and are used by more than half of the village population. They are the common meeting-ground for all classes, all sects, all sorts, all ages.

There the politician eulogises his own and deprecates the rival party; the rector meets the Nonconformists; the maiden meets her lover; the village soprano makes her public debut; the villagers first learn to trip it on the light fantastic toe; the young man plays billiards or chess, and the old man reads "The Times," the classics, or the "Weekly Dispatch."

But there are village halls and village holes! We have in Rusper, it is true, a village hall! Whereas most village or parish halls are built at the instigation or with the co-operation of the rector, our village hall at Rusper was built to keep the parson out!

This grim establishment was reared in the days of my predecessor. This good man was not invited to be a member of the committee; there seemed to be a determination to keep him out of it. To this very day it is a common boast in some corners of the village that

"The parson ain't got nothin' t' do wi' the 'all; it be the people's!"

When I first saw our village hall I shuddered; what artistic feeling there is in me was badly jarred. It is not really a hall; it is a glorified fowl house.

I have always referred to it as Madrid. As every child in a village school is aware, Madrid is the coldest capital in winter and the warmest capital in summer. And our village hall is a place where one can experience both extremes of weather.

The pious founders who ordered the hall to be built were of the opinion that it would keep the villagers away from the public-house. A worthy object indeed. Poor deluded donors! I have not yet heard that our Madrid has had any deterrent effect upon the thirsty souls of Rusper. I believe there is still good business done at our local refreshment-bars.

The whitewash had hardly dried on the walls, the paint was still sticky on the door, the interior was still aromatic of the builders' yard, when suddenly the gossips awoke to the possibilities for scandal opened up by our new Madrid.

However good were the intentions of the founders, however thoughtful they had been of the people who were likely to use it, they had not taken into account the great malady from which our population suffers.

That I should again revert to the slanderous tongue in this connection will probably cause surprise to many of my readers. I can well imagine anyone asking the natural question: "Is Rusper any worse in regard to calumny and calumniators than any other village?"

The answer is "Yes," and again "Yes." To anyone who doubts it, I suggest that he call at Rusper and test these charges of mine for himself.

I will guarantee that the first person that he meets at either Horsham or Three Bridges Station — Rusper lies between the two — will tell him of the scandal-loving nature of Rusper. And when he enters the village he will find as much evidence as he requires.

It must be remembered that the allegations were not originally made by myself; they were made by the judge — the learned man who, without bias, sat weighing the evidence at my trial.

He stated himself, for all to hear, that Rusper was a hotbed of scandal.

If my readers can adequately appreciate this cardinal truth about Rusper's propensities for scandal-mongering, for slander, gossip, and back-biting, then they will realise on what lines our parish hall soon developed.

What was to be the paradise of the village — the communal home, the place where all were to meet as brothers and sisters and on absolute equality — soon became the village scandal-shop!

Stephen Harvey must have lived in a village, and heard what things are uttered in some of our parish halls, for he writes, in "Juvenal's Satire":

> "There's a lust in man no charm can tame
> Of loudly publishing our neighbour's shame;
> On eagles' wings immortal scandals fly,
> While virtuous actions are but born to die."

The lust for scandal, the desire to publish our neighbour's shame —and if he had no shame, to invent something of which he would be ashamed — was allowed full play in our little parish hall, and the virtuous actions were ever forgot.

I can trace the origin of nearly every one of the multitude of modern slanders which haunt the houses of this quaint village to our parish hall. It is the most fertile breeding-ground for slander in England.

If slanders were spirits, the village hall of Rusper would contain enough ghosts to provide every mansion and cottage in the country with its own haunted room. What the Black Hole of Calcutta conveys to the English mind of the experiences of our people in India, the Black Hole of Rusper conveys to the mind of many of the righteous people of our village.

In our village hall, as Shakespeare has it in "Measure for Measure":

> "No might nor greatness in mortality
> Can censure 'scape; back-wounding calumny
> The whitest virtue strikes. What king so strong
> Can tie the gall up in the slanderous tongue!"

I was speaking to a brother clergyman recently about village halls, and he confessed that what was happening in my own parish was, to almost as great an extent, taking place in his own hamlet.

"What can we do to divert all this waste energy of the evil tongue to more useful purposes?" he asked.

"There is only one way," I answered. "We have to teach these people to see the mote in their own eye." And it is for that very purpose that these articles are written. If anyone should read them, and then pause before uttering a slander which might hurt and blight the life of another, I shall feel that I have done something worthy, and shall feel that my own sufferings were not in vain.

In our village hall — our cockpit, where combs are cut, when some of our ladies and gentlemen put on their spurs — both religion and politics must not be discussed, according to the rules laid down by the pious founders. Yet I have heard there things worse than politics, low and unclean though these may be at times; worse than religion, narrow and intolerant though religion sometimes may be.

I have heard noble women, who, in these village hamlets, are our Florence Nightingales or Nurse Cavells, so spoken of that my whole being has been stirred with righteous indignation. I have seen neighbours foaming with rage over such small matters as the repairing of the village pump.

I have seen spinsters and married women without families wildly gesticulating and shouting that if they had forty sons they would give every one of them to their country. I remember how one son of the soil interpolated: "Why, they ain't got no sons!" — to the amusement of myself and the others in the meeting. I know the bitter tears that have been made to flow in my own home, and many others, because of the evil utterances that have been made in this parish hall.

Painful and amusing are the stories that I could tell of this village hall. But, like the Madrid of Spain, there is hope for it yet. I can see the day coming when the cobwebs of scandal shall be brushed away, when these papers, read by its habitues, have been assimilated and their advice followed, when it shall become the true settlement of the village; and brotherly love and mutual toleration shall flourish where until recently venomous gossip thrust forth its deadly forked tongue.

CHAPTER XVII

JUMBLE SALES AND JUMBLED PEOPLE

There is one day in the village year when busy tongues are too much occupied with other things to give voice to scandal. Consequently, many of us look forward to that as a red-letter day. It is the day of the annual Jumble Sale!

Jumble Sale Day is to a village very much like Independence Day is to America. It is a kind of Coronation Day, Jubilee Day, Peace Day, and Harvest Home all in one.

Our villages have no Harrod's Stores or Selfridge's; no big emporiums where we can unburden ourselves of our weekly surplus. We have only the Jumble Sale to look forward to. For this great event we patiently save our sixpences and shillings, and count the passing days until the auspicious occasion arrives. There is no fixed day for the holding of Rusper's great Jumble Sale.

It may take place at any time, though it must be held once a year. The date is usually determined by the state of the wardrobes of our local Dives.

If there have been some remarkable sales in Oxford Street or Kensington, and some of the wealthy ladies of the parish have returned to the village accompanied by huge "bargain bundles," and by husbands with quince-like expressions, due to depleted pockets, then we know that a Jumble Sale is imminent.

"Mrs. So-and-So has worn a new dress every day this week!" remarks one of our observant village women to a neighbour. "Shall we urge forward the sale?"

The neighbour thinks that it is nearly time, and so the Jumble

Sale movement begins.

There is no difficulty in collecting certain articles for the "jumble." One reason may be that we have no local pawnbroker! A van is sent round the parish to garner in the "fallen stars" of the wardrobes. I have seen, and sighed over, the collections that ultimately reach our Village Hall for the great sale. They comprise clothing in the very last stages of decay, furniture lacking legs and knobs, saucepans and pails which will never again hold water, and ornaments as chipped as they are ugly.

Of course, there are also many very valuable and useful personal and household articles contained in the Jumble Sale gifts. Some of the men and women of the village display generosity and self-denial which makes me proud to be their minister. I know it to be a fact that some give what they really cannot spare.

Their action is in agreement with their whole mode of life; they are the true servants of Christ, and as freely as they have received so are they ready freely to give.

One day I called at a widow's cottage, at the same time that the Jumble Sale van was in her neighbourhood. She was looking at two coal-scuttles, one of which she used in her parlour, and the other in the kitchen.

"I think that I can spare one of these," she said to me rather wistfully. "It is about all that I can give, but I feel that I should like to do something for a good cause."

The widow was volunteering a mighty mite! As I reflected upon what was sent from some of the big houses, I felt constrained to say that, in my opinion, the cause was not so impelling as to justify the acceptance of a gift which would impoverish a widow's sparsely-furnished home.

There is more real treasure represented, both in earth and heaven, in that humble coal-scuttle than in some of the houses of the well-stocked wardrobes from which the rags are sent to be sold to Lazarus and his household!

Rusper's Jumble Sale is famed far and near. Not only do all the parishioners turn up at the great auction, but strangers come in from miles around. And their bicycles, their pony-traps and donkey-carts make our quiet old street resemble a corner of Mitcham or Leipzig Fairs. So busy are the sales-ladies and purchasers in driving their bargains within, and so busy are the donkeys braying without, that for once there is no time and apparently little inclination for the distilling of scandal.

One curious thing that I have noticed about our Jumble Sale is that some of the best garments appear and reappear. The first year they are purchased by persons a grade lower than those who gave them, and, having been worn by them for twelve months, are sent on to the next Jumble Sale.

I have in mind now one such dress which has already been thrice sold, and I still meet it in my rambles. It will be back again, I feel sure, at the next "Jumble Scramble." If the business house that turned out this imperishable creation could send a representative to see it, a valuable advertisement might be secured.

One of the bargains which was once obtained at our "Jumble" was a beehive. Unfortunately for the purchaser, sufficient care had not been taken to dispossess all the original bee occupants of the hive. On his way home, I am informed, the proud possessor unwittingly jolted his "living overweight" into hostile activity — and discovered that tongues were not the only things which can sting in this district!

When first I came to Rusper these Jumble Sales were held to obtain church expenses. From the day of my arrival I objected, from the highest motives, to this form of raising money for religious purposes. I have always contended that a church, whose congregation is by no means destitute, should be supported by voluntary contributions, not by the hawking of greasy clothes and tattered linen. My present churchwardens have taken a bold stand on this matter, and nowadays the proceeds of the Jumble Sales go to some worthy object elsewhere.

There was one "result" of the Jumble Sales which slightly disturbed me at first. After one of these general re-shuffles of old clothes, I had only barely prevented myself from bowing to the wrong people!

I have dealt with Jumble Sales with more levity than I intended, but the object at the back of my mind has been to deprecate sales of old clothing. Those who have enough and to spare ought to give freely of their abundance, and those unfortunates who have insufficient should not be asked for money when presented with old clothing. And to support a church on the proceeds of the sale of rags and bones is, to me, unthinkable!

CHAPTER XVIII

THOSE WHO STAYED AT HOME

The war revealed to anyone with eyes to see the real character of the people in Rusper, as, indeed, in every other English village.

The best men left our village, and many did not return. The worst men — and these included some professedly pious — lagged behind and displayed great zeal and ingenuity in dodging the Army.

My church, which was packed with young men on Sunday evenings, soon became depleted; the majority entered the Army, the others were too ashamed to enter the church and meet the clergyman whose strong views on the war and whose outspokenness were well known to them.

For some of the young men who stayed behind I had genuine sympathy, particularly for the only sons of poor widows.

One maiden lady of means, I remember, once addressed a recruiting meeting in our village hall, and, fastening her gaze upon one young man who was the sole support of many near relatives, was openly caustic about his dilatoriness in joining up.

Another wealthy old maid loudly declared that she would have given all her sons to fight for the country, and seemed rather perturbed when a rustic jeeringly reminded her, amid laughter, that "You ain't got any sons, missus!"

Before advising any one of our villagers to answer the call I took steps to offer my own services to the country; I had worn a tunic for six years, and I preferred a khaki coat to a coat of arms from the Heralds' Office, and. was ready at any moment to exchange the girdle of my cassock for a Sam Browne belt. I could handle a rifle, and hit a bulls-eye at one thousand yards.

The result of my application to the War Office I have already detailed in the chapter on "My Farming Adventures." Having volunteered my own services, I had a satisfactory answer for anyone who asked me about myself when I was urging our villagers to follow the Flag.

Rusper's response was creditable. We sent 120 men out of a total population of 620, and, I am glad to say, only a few of those 120 had to be fetched.

But there were others who ought to have been fetched. Some were among the poorest in the village before the war. Our noble, clean-living young gallants who joined early used to feel it a condescension, I believe, to speak to some of those very lowly-placed slackers before the war.

But, alas and alack! now that the heroes have come back they have discovered that these self-same lowly people they used to know and, possibly, despise have soared almost to the heights of Olympus.

These stay-at-homes saw the chance of making money, and making it quickly, and so, while they were safely protected by the shilling-a-day Tommy who had nobly left his job open for them, they awoke and got busy. And now the returned hero is lucky if he is recognised by our newly-rich.

Before the war our newly-rich could hardly write their names — they had never seen a cheque-book; now their names are written on the licences of their motor-cars, if not on the roll of honour.

I watched our village slackers perfecting themselves in the art of dodging military service. Some of them were helped by Messrs. Dives, their employers. Contemptible were the methods they used. When I recall these matters, and think of the hell through which our village heroes went, I feel embittered and ashamed.

I saw men who had never handled a spade, who could not tell you how to dig a rod of ground, become proficient and indispensable gardeners in a fleeting night. I saw some of the fancy gardeners change in a twinkling to agricultural labourers by the simple method of planting potatoes in a flower-bed, and

I felt that even "the heathen Chinese" could not have shown himself more adaptable and adroit.

I saw — though not in my own parish, I'm glad to say — horse-dealers become farmers and gamekeepers change to swineherds and poultry-farmers in less time than it took for Jonah's gourd to spring up and perish.

While our boys fought, these men of military age and a new calling began to make their pile. Men who used to speak of pence with bated breath, as do the Scottish, now talk airily of pounds, and are developing a corporation!

Some small farmers who only had a few lean goats, have now a herd of fine cows. And the crowning irony of-all is that the dodgers are laughing at those whom they describe as "the fools who went out to fight."

As I wander round my parish I meet some of our shattered men who have come back to us in parts, and when they tell me what they have noticed, and how they have been described as "fools," I remind them of the "fool" of the Bible, who waxed so fat and prosperous that he decided to pull down his barns and build greater ones, but was thus answered: "Thou fool, this night shall thy soul be required of thee."

I tell them that before God and man I would sooner by far be the bearer of their noble scars, and endure their daily torment through lost limbs, than be one of the fortunate and jeering men who failed at the time of "the great test." Those unhappy people who failed once may fail again at the next, and perhaps the final, test; but the already half-forgotten village heroes now know the sweets of soul-serenity which come to all who, forgetful of self, do their bit as a sacred duty to their country and to God.

Who would think that after the remarkable, emotional wave which passed over our towns and villages when war began, that it should be necessary, within less than six years, to call public attention to jesting at our returned heroes by the slackers who have reaped where they did not sow, and gathered where they have not strawed!

One little incident that comes back to me now of those early war days happened at the medical examination which I underwent when trying to enter the Army.

The Army doctor said that I was sound in mind and limb, and then added: "But what is this that is tattooed on your chest?" He pointed to an Irish Celtic Cross, my M.A. degree, and the date of my ordination, which were tattooed on my body. I explained that in the far-off days of the seventh century it was the custom among Irish missionaries to wear a cross on their flesh, and I explained that my call to preach the Cross and its power was to me something more than a vow; it was undertaken after I had received a vision, and I was prepared to preach it in khaki as well as in a cassock.

But I was rejected in deference to the canons of tho Church!

CHAPTER XIX

A LITTLE BIT OF HEAVEN

During the five years that I have spent in this village hell I touched, I remember, and am devoutly grateful for it, just "a little bit of heaven."

This patch of Paradise was not in Rusper, but about five miles away. It was not, as some may think, a beauty spot, or one of those delightful establishments where all members of a fine family, placed in affluent circumstances, order their lives on the Christian ideal, and make their home a little heaven to any and every visitor.

Such homes and families, fortunately, are to be found even in my scandal-haunted parish of Rusper, as elsewhere. My "little bit of heaven" was neither picturesque nor luxurious; it was a gaunt, drab military camp — the Artillery Camp at Roffey, near Horsham.

There, among men — real men, who have no use for women in a clergyman's cassock — I was happy.

These magnificent young men required the religion that would appeal to youth and strength; that would succour and console them when meeting a powerful enemy with fixed bayonets. What did they care whether I burned the right-smelling incense or turned the exact number of degrees towards the east?

They did not look down at my boots and say that, because they were protected by a few useful hobnails or a couple of Blakey's, I was defiling the house of God and standing between them and the blessing from above.

Though they were very attentive to their own uniform they

never wrote me letters complaining that I wore the wrong colours; they were too well disciplined to stand up during the service and say that we were singing an unusual hymn, or to ask me to pronounce the Absolution the second time.

Nor did they fight for the best pews, nor thrust out their tongues at the other worshippers, as was the custom among some of my own parishioners. They did not sweep out of the church looking with contempt on the other less affluent members of the congregation. And, what is far more to the point, they did not forget the straight, homely Christian teachings. What a contrast it all was! After one of my own services at Rusper some of the superior people would drive home in their motor-cars and set their telephones working to inform their friends of the language used by their own "village Father Vaughan."

The wires would work and the tongues would wag. "We must write again to the bishop about him. Do you know, my dear, he actually went and milked his cows before coming to Holy Communion this morning!" These and similar declamations would pass along the wires to listening ears, greedy for the latest gossip and scandal.

At my "little bit of heaven" how different it all was! Before I could get away from the camp the khaki-clad fellows would press round me and firmly grasp me by the hand and say how much they had been helped by my straightforward discourse. How could I help contrasting this reception with that at Rusper?

It was in 1916 that I was first asked to preach at the newly-founded Roffey Camp, late on Saturday evening. I was rung up on the telephone and asked to preach the following morning. Before agreeing — and I was anxious to accept — I put my cob, Kitty, in the trap and called on the Vicar of Roffey.

There is, it must be understood, an etiquette amongst the Anglican clergy that permission should be asked of the local clergyman before entering his parish to take a duty. The vicar consented. His church, where, the services had previously been held, was too small, and the services were now held in the large Y.M.C.A. hut. I was asked to come again.

During the week, however, I heard that several chaplains had been recently dismissed from this camp, and I was strongly advised against taking up duty there, as I might be up against some of the blood-and-thunder type of officer. I was officiating clergyman to the camp for a whole year, and only resigned when it was clear that I was no follower of the great Calvin, who, though a reformer, theologian, and writer, yet held the untenable doctrine that men were predestined, from the foundation of the world to eternal heaven or eternal hell.

Sunday morning services at the camp were attended by the Church of England men. The men of "fancy religions," as the sergeant-major described them, went outside to Horsham. These Sunday morning services were hours of pure joy to me. I apologised on one occasion for the length of my sermon — I had been speaking half an hour — when several men shouted out: "Go on!" I reminded them to have mercy on my cob, Kitty, who had to take me back five miles in twenty-five minutes, to my own service.

I had to sell Kitty to pay for my trial. She has now returned. She was a favourite at the camp; she got all the spare sugar and carrots. One admirer pulled enough hair out of her tail and mane to make a watchchain; another sent a lock of her hair to his girl! Like myself, he had not many curls of his own to spare from his shiny scalp.

I could not fall inline with some of my parishioners, but I fell in line with the Tommies.

The officers came and asked me if they could bring their wives to the service. I allowed no fair ladies from Rusper to come, however. The men on fatigue duty stole in to the service; they all wanted to hear "Big Paddy" as they affectionately called me.

Great was my astonishment when scores of these men walked out from the camp five miles to my service one Sunday evening. I noticed a pew filled with officers. As it was a wet night I was anxious to ask them to my house for supper, and curious to know why they came so far.

They told me that they had been at the morning service at the camp. To use their own words: "The service had bucked them up." They were leaving next day for the Front, and they wanted to come to hear me once more. One of these officers was a bishop's son, who had sent notes of my sermons to his father.

These men were Canadians, from all parts of the great

Dominion. Many were married, and had left their wives and children behind. Only those who have been in a far-off land know what home-sickness is, particularly on Sunday afternoon.

To the home-sick I gave a special invitation. My house was like Barnardo's Homes, open night and day.

I urged my congregation to open their houses and entertain the sons of the Maple Leaf, but I failed in this. Soldiers don't talk scandal; if medals were awarded for slander they might have had a hot joint instead of the cold shoulder!

During the last three months of my work at the camp, Rusper was put out of bounds. One of the scandal-mongers of my parish wrote to the War Office complaining that soldiers made a disturbance in the village by singing songs.

When I reflect on my work at Rusper the Furies seem to dance on my midnight pillow, for every good work I have attempted to carry out has been frustrated by some local slander-monger and anonymous letter-writer.

On one occasion I brought my trap full of rabbits to the boys at the camp. The next day I had an anonymous letter to say that the next time I took rabbits to the camp I might catch them on my own farm! Had I known the writer or writers, my reply might have been that I should ask the soldiers at the camp to take a few tongues as scalps from Rusper the next time they called.

The only defection from discipline I have known amongst the Canadians at Roffey was a row in a public-house in Horsham. I was passing through the town, and the military police told me there was serious trouble.

One of the combatants was known to me. I met him years ago as ticket-collector on the boat that crosses Lake Ontario from Toronto to Leweston, Niagara. He had been at my house the previous Sunday. I called out in a stentorian voice: "Fall in — tallest on the right, shortest on the left!" The noise ceased, and several cried out: "Here's our padre, Big Paddy!" I asked for a cane, but they refused to hold out their hands.

I have heard from many of those splendid lads, but there are some no man can hear from, for they, have poured out the rich wine of life on the fields of Flanders. Some were rough diamonds, I know, but they were white inside, and in ministering to them I found my "little bit of heaven."

CHAPTER XX

BAITING THE PARSON

Parish work in a country village is not a joy-row in a Cleopatra barge made of gold and ivory, with purple sails; a long dream of fragrance and song, luxury and music, Arcadian days and nights. On the contrary, it is more like a pilgrimage in penitential clothes, a penance for deeds that have never been done.

The amenities of village life are few. One misses the sweet converse with the intellectual minds which are numerous in towns but sparse in villages. To the man who has no resources in himself village life becomes like a stagnant pool.

I miss the friendship of kindred minds in this country village. Often have I, in the confessional of my own mind, debated again and again whether the words uttered by a pious priest at my ordination were true.

He affirmed that every man has a deep in his own heart answering to the deep of God. Certainly, as I look around and measure the methods of my parishioners, from the village toper, who whispers gossip and slander and spite, to the sleek philosopher who lolls on his soft cushions, who ransacks the Bible for promises for himself and for curses for his neighbour, I wonder if I am right in continuing my career in this picturesque old village.

When the first warnings of persecution were sounded, some of my clerical and lay friends advised me to put my money in my pocket, my effects on my back, and leave the sow to wallow in the mire. They urged me to do as Our Lord advised:

"And whosoever shall not receive you, nor hear your words, when ye depart out of that house or city, shake off the dust of your feet.

"Verily, I say unto you, it shall be more tolerable for the land of Sodom and Gomorrah in the day of judgment than for that city."

Among some of the Nonconformist denominations it is a custom for their ministers to move on after they have spent three years in one circuit. Sometimes they go before that time. I have heard of some extraordinary Nonconformist ministers and unusual congregations who have declared against the three-year system.

There is one case that I have in mind where a congregation threatened to break away from their denomination unless their minister, whom they had grown to love, were allowed to remain indofinitely, It required a special resolution of their Church Conference to meet this case, but the resolution was passed, and the minister remained.

Needless to say, that minister was not labouring amongst a village flock. His church was in one of the largest towns in England. In that town there were theatres, sports grounds, public libraries, public baths, an aquarium, trams, 'buses, and every other diversion common to a large town, but rarely, if ever, seen in a village.

Thus the people of that town had sufficient natural entertainment and diversion without having to turn, as a village first turns, to its parson, and invents scandals as to his mode of life, as an enjoyable pastime.

This passion for gossip and scandal seems to be an echo of the old customs of ancient Rome. We have become more civilised nowadays, and the Government will not allow the apostles of Christ to be sent into the arena, while the populace revel in the death agonies of these human sacrifices.

But the blood-thirst still survives among our village populations. Kipling writes, with telling effect, of the Chicago woman, clothed in scarlet, who used to attend the slaughterhouses of the Beef Trust to watch the blood flowing from the dumb, dying cattle.

I have seen some village women so insensitive to pain in animals that they enjoy watching the butcher's knife as it is thrust into the squealing pig. But their pleasure is still greater when they watch others thrust, or themselves thrust, the knife of scandal into their parson.

What the sacrifices of Christians were to the populace of ancient Rome so is the mental anguish of a clergyman to some of the women of the English villages. The chief difference is, that whereas in Rome the unfortunate persons who were thrust into the arena to die were despatched the same afternoon, either in the arena or outside in the shambles, the village parson must live on to endure the tortures caused by the poisoned tongues.

Sometimes I am asked why do I only, of all ordained ministers, write and speak as I do of the anguish caused to me by the voice of scandal. And my questioners assume that as others are silent they do not suffer.

I challenge any reader of these articles to put the question to any minister of religion he knows, and to ask him if he has not had to suffer silently, even as I suffer, without being silent, through the base inventions of some persons to whom he ministers.

Every clerical friend I have has told me that he has had, at some time or other, similar things alleged about him as have from time to time been fastened on to me. And they suffer on in silence, or leave the locality and their unworthy traducers for fresh fields in which to labour.

Since my first article appeared I have had hundreds of letters from clergymen, who have expressed to me their pleasure at the exposure of the cruel treatment meted out to the priests by their parishioners.

It is very remarkable that within a radius of eight miles from Rusper there is not one clergyman who has endured his parish for more than five years.

When I was in Canada I was told that the most contemptible name given to a man was "Quitter"; it was a synonym for a man who had not the endurance for his job.

In Dante's Inferno there is a special circle for the cowards; they are placed in the limbo of oblivion as unworthy to make progress.

I felt that I would be a coward if I turned back in the day of trouble. The great general at Thermopylae dismissed his five thousand cowards, and held the pass against Alexander with three hundred men.

Any cowardly thoughts I had I dismissed, knowing that one of the greatest things to fight for is a good name.

And that is the reason why I stay on at Rusper. I will not be turned out of my holy office, or be prevented from serving my Maker, by the cowardly voice of the calumniator.

Rusper Church in 1905 from the Knight Album

CHAPTER XXI

VILLAGE SCROOGES

I met Mr. and Mrs. Scrooge, Miss Scrooge, and all the little Scrooges very early in my ministry at Rusper. They were perfect replicas of the grasping old fossil discovered by Dickens when he wrote his famous Christmas story.

When I was first introduced to our local Scrooges, I rubbed my eyes and asked myself whether I was living in a Sussex village in modern England, or back in those harsh days which Dickens pictured so vividly.

I had frequently heard that the people of the southern counties of England were famed for meanness, inhospitality, and uncharitableness. I did not believe it until I came to live at Rusper. I refused to believe it, because I had previously discovered for myself that similar charges against other communities were grossly untrue.

Before I paid my first visit to Scotland I was under the impression that the residents in Caledonia, stern and wild, were also mean and inhospitable. I speedily discovered that the reverse is the case. No more good-hearted, generous people can be found anywhere than among the Highlands and Lowlands of Scotland.

In fact, it was not until I came to Rusper, when 1 had passed my prime of life, that I met my first genuine Scrooge, but I found him here — the real uncamouflaged article; the man with, the heart of stone, the woman with the clutching hand.

Scrooge and his wife and family do not live in one isolated house; they live here on my right, there on my left, yonder over the sunlit hill, and down there towards the green vale. The fingers of my two hands are too few on which to count them; I should require a large notebook for an adequate enumeration.

Mr. Scrooge saw Marley's ghost, and Scrooge ceased to screw his employés and his customers. He grew to be as generous as he once was mean.

There are ghosts in Rusper village, and in most other villages, if local superstitions are to be believed. Once I was invited to sit up all night and lay a ghost in this district. But the common or garden ghost is not the kind of spirit that is needed in these parts. We want ghosts a la Scrooge's deceased partner, Marley.

If the spirits of a hundred departed Marleys could return to this locality and disturb the slumbers of some of our heartless money-grubbers — those worshippers of the golden calf who spend their sordid evenings nursing or perusing their fattening bankbooks — we might see a parish of regenerated men and women, who would delight in good deeds even as did the original Scrooge after he saw the third apparition.

Scrooge No. 1, as I must call him, because he would be aggrieved if I published his real name, impatiently listened to me when I called upon him with a pitiable tale of the plight of one of the men in his employ. I described to him the sorry conditions of this poor fellow's home, spoke of the empty fire-grate and the coalless cellar.

I suggested that his employé was worthy of his hire, that, as the result of his day's toil, he should at least have the satisfaction of knowing that the occupants of his home had the necessaries of life. Scrooge No. 1 tried to stop me pouring out my true tale, but I persisted.

Standing in his luxurious drawing-room before a blazing fire on that cold winter's morning, he told me that he had too many things to think about to listen to stories of the domestic life of his workmen. If the man wasn't satisfied with the twenty-odd shillings a week that he was being paid — well, let him go to someone who would pay him more.

And some of our big employers are to-day assuming the air of martyrs because labour, united, is putting on the screw. It is the unfeeling attitude of unjust employers such as this Scrooge No. 1 that is largely responsible for the excessive demands that some organised workers are beginning to make.

Rusper's Parish Magazine was twelve pounds in debt when I arrived. So I called on some of the wealthy women in my congregation. "Money for a 'magazine! Whatever next, my dear Rector!" said Mrs. Scrooge. Of course she could not think of contributing to remove such a debt, and she had no more time to spare that morning, as she was running up to town for a day's shopping. From Mrs. Scrooge No. 1 I went to Mrs. Scrooge No. 2, and so on, and always received the same kind of reception.

I was about to call on the remaining few when I stopped and asked myself: Why should a clergyman have to waste his time soliciting money from these ungenerous parishioners? I did not continue that tour. I went back to the rectory, wrote a cheque on my own bank, and paid off the debt at one stroke.

And that was the end of Rusper's Church Magazine, for I determined then that a publication which required such humiliating efforts from its rector-editor was a luxury better dispensed with. And I do not think our church or parish has suffered from its disappearance.

There are many stories that I should like to tell of those who were content to give nothing, or to give only a bad halfpenny. I remember calling one morning on a wealthy woman to enlist her sympathies and to obtain some financial help for our Church Lads' Brigade.

This woman kept me at her large establishment all the morning while she crowed aloud of the unique beauties of her flowers, her bric-a-brac, and her live stock. Patiently I listened, longing to collect her subscription and to get back to my other duties. But she babbled on.

If my Church lads only knew what a great effort I was making to please this dear old lady so that she might condescend to give of her abundance for their benefit! There were only the pigs to be seen when I made another valiant effort to secure a subscription.

But no, I *must* see the pigs! So we wandered down to the sty and surveyed the young porkers. I praised them, too — their colour, their size, their ears and intelligent eyes, their curly tails, and wiry bristles — and then we got back to the Church Lads' Brigade. After all those strenuous hours during that long and memorable morning I left with —sixpence!

I called on one gentleman near my church, and he sent out to say that I would greatly oblige him if I followed in the footsteps of my wise predecessor and left him alone.

One week-end some members of a Church deputation came to our village. We were then full up at the rectory, and I asked some of my congregation if they would offer hospitality to our Church visitors. Some of those that were well able to do so refused, and it was only after making many calls that at last I found someone willing to receive our Church guests.

One worthy soul, in high dudgeon, turned into her house without speaking another word, and slammed her door in my face. I am afraid there is no danger of an angel being entertained unawares in that inhospitable home.

One bitter day, when many of the cottagers were freezing because there was no coal in the village, I saw some coal carts, heavily laden with coal, on the way to some of the big houses.

I had already been warned that the rector was not allowed to cut down the trees at his rectory. The circumstances of that warning were, to speak euphemistically, rather peculiar.

I was walking down my drive one morning, when I heard someone whistling. I looked round, and I saw a church member beckoning rather excitedly. Thinking there was something the matter, I walked back, and was greeted thus: "D'ye see these trees here?" I admitted that it was difficult to avoid seeing them. "Well, please understand this," he proceeded — "we don't allow our rectors to cut those down."

For a moment I was speechless. I was new to the parish and village ways at that time. At first I thought that this whistling member was joking, or suffering from a slight mental aberration. Only so could I understand this gratuitous insult.

When I realised that he was really in earnest, I pointed to the shops in the village, and asked him why he did not whistle me to tell me that Rusper did not allow its rector to throw stones at those windows or to steal apples or eggs.

I thought of this strange interview when I saw some of the villagers freezing through lack of coals. And I went straightaway and bought a saw, cut down as much wood as I could, sawed it into logs, and distributed it among them, saying to myself as I did so: "I'll risk the consequences."

Of the stinginess of some of the villagers when soldiers came through the village; of the opposition I encountered when trying to arrange for the distribution of buns and cigarettes; of the man who refused to send some brandy to a dying woman; of the morning collections, when the offertory totalled sometimes less than a shilling; of the special collections which I had to make up to avoid public shame, I could write chapters.

But I am too ashamed to say more.

CHAPTER XXII

SERMONS THAT GAVE OFFENCE

As the months dragged past, and the village tongues wagged further and faster, I found it necessary to be more outspoken in my weekly sermons.

After an unusually ingenuous and plain-spoken discourse some of the white souls in my congregation, with tears in their pious eyes, would come to me and express their gratitude for the spiritual help and consolation they had received. Others, who had been touched to the quick by my uncompromising language, came to me and, speaking with scarcely-suppressed anger, bitterly denounced my sermons and my bold language.

Sometimes I was tempted to utter the natural retort about wearing the cap which obviously fitted, but I did not do so. I felt deep down in my soul a great pity for the poor blind Pharisees, who were wilfully shutting out the clear light which might have illuminated and clarified their darkened souls.

In those far-off days in the Holy Land Christ was made to lament that they would not come to Him so that they might have life. He was captiously questioned and criticised by certain antagonists in his congregations; and I was content to answer the critics politely, although sometimes I feel moved to righteous indignation, and to describe them, as Our Lord described, his taunters, as a generation of vipers. As Defoe says in "The True-Born Englishman":

"Wherever God erects a house of prayer,
The Devil always builds a chapel there,

And 'twill be found upon examination
The latter always has the larger congregation."

Before I came to Rusper I had heard many complaints of the general debility of sermons, and critics spoke caustically of the somniferous style, of discourses that aimed at nothing and hit it — hard, of sermons that were lifeless and dead, of sermons that were a river of words containing a spoonful of thought. And so I determined that none should ever accuse me of producing such as these.

I do not suggest that the parson is always to blame when the eyes of many of his congregation close in slumber, and their heads begin to lose their perpendicular. Even an inspired apostle like St. Paul could not keep all of his congregation awake, for we read that when he preached far into the night one of his congregation — Eutychus — dropping asleep fell from the third gallery into the theatre below — dead!

No one has ever yet accused me of making my sermons dull. My offence was that I was too interesting, too arresting, too forceful, too disturbing to those who do not like to see the covering of whitewash removed from the black stains in their daily life.

The advice that was being constantly tendered me, that I should preach milk-and-water sermons, instead of the real juice of the vine, I regarded in the same way as a medical man regards the quack. I had taken my degree, and passed the theological examinations. I preferred to rely upon what I had learned from my skilled pastors and masters, to accepting Mother Some-body's herbal tonic or Grandfather Somebody's soothing syrup.

There is one weakness of an Irish friend of mine which I have not been guilty of. This priest consistently mistakes perspiration for inspiration. I disapprove of sermons knocked in by sheer physical force. I do not bang the Bible or bruise my wrist on the pulpit.

Before I came to Rusper I had earned a reputation as a preacher. I could draw and hold a crowd, and the columns of at least five religious papers were always open to publish my sermons. Thus it came as a shock to find amateur theologians of this village set on a hill, which cannot be hid, endeavouring

95

to instruct me as to how to preach. To an unbiased mind it would seem just as preposterous for an untrained man to attempt to instruct a sky pilot as for a carter to attempt to teach an air pilot.

I would have been refreshed to have heard the answers that my advisers would have received had they, instead of proffering me their advice, gone to their dentist and instructed him as to the best way of pulling out teeth, or tried to initiate their baker into the mysteries of scientific bread-making.

Byron says:

"Good but rarely comes from good advice."

And Dryden, in "The Cock and the Fox," says:

"An honest man may take a knave's advice,
But idiots only may be cozened twice.
Once warned is well bewared."

Why, I feel that I am entitled to ask, should a mere tyro attempt to proffer advice to a man who has graduated in theology, the queen of sciences?

I have preached only practical Christianity, not points of ritual or points of Biblical interpretation. I have preached as a living man to living men; as one of the people, not as a man set apart and above his parishioners, and certainly not as a dying man to dying men.

My creed is that a man has no more religion — no matter what he professes; no matter what are his doctrines and dogmas — than he puts into practice. He can swallow everything in the Bible, in the Prayer Book, in all creeds, and in all hymn books, and in all devotional works. Yet his real religion is written in his daily life. And that is what I have been trying to get into the heads of the Christians of Rusper; and because I have done so in season and out of season, in the green days and the dry days, I have been made to suffer mental martyrdom surely as great and agonising as the physical pains of one of the martyrs of the early Christian era.

After one of my encounters with the amateur theologians, I

turned up both Longfellow and Lowell. I read through Longfellow's "Courtship of Miles Standish," and discovered these lines:

"Look I You can see from this window my brazen howitzer planted
High on the roof of the church, a preacher who speaks to the purpose,
Steady, straightforward, and strong, with irresistible logic;
Orthodox, flashing conviction right into the hearts of the heathen.
   .   .   .   .
Truly the only tongue that is understood by the savage
Must be the tongue of fire that speaks from the mouth of the cannon!"

As I read I became more and more convinced that the only tongue that could be understood here, where tongues were long and busy as the bees, was the tongue of burning fire. I felt that I must go on and preach hard, unpalatable truths, and try to be as tho man outlined in Lowell's "Fable for Critics":

"This is what makes him the crowd-drawing preacher:
There's a background of God to each hard-working feature,
Every word that he speaks has been fiercely furnaced
In the blast of a life that has struggled in earnest.
   .   .   .   .
But his periods fall on you, stroke after stroke,
Like the blows of a lumberer felling an oak.
You forget the man wholly, you're thankful to meet
With a preacher who smacks of the field and the street."

That "I smack of the field and the street" is undoubted, that I have been "fiercely furnaced" all the world now knows.

I continued to assert in my sermons that we may erect orthodox boundaries, print manuals on devotions, build temples which will one day become ruins, erect tablets which will crumble to dust; but if we wrote not on the fleshly tablets the love of right and truth, the hatred of wrong and lies, we were but hypocrites of the same type as those who criticised and put to death the Man of Galilee.

My critics, observing that I was not adapting myself to their ideas, wrote often to the bishop to complain of my sermons. One of these busy scribes overstepped himself on one occasion. When the late Suffragan Bishop, of happy memory, who was a man as well as a bishop, wrote and asked me to call and see him on a rather important matter, I assumed immediately that this important matter was a stab in the back from one of my letter-writing critics.

I was right! The bishop told me that a sermon I had preached on behalf of the Queen Victoria Clergy Fund had caused annoyance, and asked me kindly to let him see it. Great was his surprise and amusement — in which I joined — to discover that this was one of the few sermons that I have preached which was not original. It was the sermon of a well-known bishop and historical scholar, and was originally delivered to an appreciative congregation in — Westminster Abbey!

An interpolation in one of my sermons which caused great offence was that, though I was a University man and had married a lady, I earned during my first year at Rusper the magnificent sum of 2s. 10½d per day — less than three-half-pence an hour!

My rule in preaching is not iron-cast. I invariably preach according to the Church year. I have preached on the subjects of All Saints' Day, All Souls' Day, and, owing to the behaviour of some of my parishioners, when the First of April came round, I found it necessary, if not diplomatic, to preach on "All Fools' Day." This was one of the sermons that gave the greatest offence.

After the sermon, one of my congregation sent me a verse from Kipling's "Vampire," and suggested that I should quote it in my next sermon. Why he sent it to me I cannot yet understand. This was the verse:

"A fool there was, and he made his prayer
(Even as you and I)
To a rag and a bone and a hank of hair
(We called her the woman who did not care);

But the fool, he called her his lady fair
(Even as you and I)."

Possibly this poor parishioner was not too happily married! I have heard of persons being angered by neighbours who play the piano badly at all hours; I have heard of some who have sent next door a brochure on "How to Play the Piano" as a friendly hint; but I had to wait until I came to Rusper before one of the bachelors in my congregation sent me a brochure on "How to Speak Effectively," giving at the same time a list of subjects on which I might discourse. When I was at another church I was once urged by a Churchman to preach a sermon on "How to be happy though married." Having hunted through my repertoire of sermons, I found the remains of this old discourse, and delivered it on the following Sunday to, among others, *the bachelor who had sent me the brochure!*

Sermons are not like postage-stamps, only to be used once. I have a hardy annual which I preach once a year. To my immediate friends I give notice of the day on which I propose to preach it, and some retort that I need not expect them on that occasion.

I call this sermon by a dual name — "Vanity in Religion" and "The Telephone Sermon." Private persons have re-delivered this sermon by telephone all over the country; others have besought me for a copy. I am hoping to have in the Press six of my sermons that gave offence, but I shall give my present readers a few excerpts from this sermon, which has brought on my head the wrath of vengeance.

"Vanity in Religion."
In this sermon I stated that the great political economist, Adam Smith, spoke of vanity as the most contemptible and ridiculous vice. I stated that the Psalmist had this same idea in his mind when he wrote, "I hate vain thoughts." Vanity in religion, I declared, was anything which courted admiration, anything which prompted the test question: "Is it religion or yourself that is uppermost in your mind?"

Vanity in religion, I emphasised, was the next-door neighbour to hypocrisy; the more ornate the ritual, the more elaborate the service, the farther we were removed from Our Lord, Who said: "God is a Spirit, and they that worship Him must worship Him in Spirit and in truth." I spoke of vanity in baptism — the vanity of names of godparents; vanity at the confirmation service; vanity in weddings, and vanity in funerals.

To this sermon more than to any other single factor I trace most of the troubles and tribulations through which myself and my family have been made to pass during these modern and supposedly more enlightened days.

"All offences," as Shakespeare says, "come from the heart," and it was the offended heart that rejected my telling talks on "Vanity in Religion."

I hope to preach that sermon at Rusper again at an early date. And I shall continue to preach this sermon year by year until the end comes, because I know it to be the unvarnished truth; because the opposition to it is the most convincing testimony to its efficacy.

CHAPTER XXIII

VILLAGE VANITIES

There are human peacocks in Hyde Park on Sunday mornings; there are birds of paradise in Bond Street; there are human apes at Court functions; there are West End boudoirs containing more mirrors than modesty — yea, London is full of pride and vanity.

Though the pride of the town-dweller and the suburbanite is proverbial, yet for the real goods — pride's essence, unadulter-ated, flamboyant, and unashamed — there is nothing comparable with the village product — and Rusper is surely the vainest of all the vain villages in England.

Pope says:

> "In pride, in reas'ning pride, our error lies;
> All quit their sphere, and rush into the skies.
> Pride still is aiming at the blessed abodes;
> Men would be angels, angels would be gods."

Our village peacocks and birds of paradise, it is true, are not such gorgeous creatures as those we see reflecting back the morning sun in Rotten Row. But they think that they are, and act as though they were the most exquisite of all the creatures of the Creator.

Yesterday I saw two of our village birds of paradise advancing towards each other down Rusper's High (and only) Street. As they sighted each other they arched their necks and spread out their brilliant plumage.

101

"My dear, how positively charming you look to-day!" said Bird of Paradise No. 1, and then waited for her friend to say the same, and more, of her own stylish but unbecoming new gown.

"And you look perfectly lovely — absolutely exquisite!" answered No. 2. After a few more words, including the latest piece of Rusper scandal, they parted, one sailing majestically down the Faygate Road and the other sweeping gaily along the Horsham highway.

But it is not of village dress that I would write as indicative of village vanities. The people of the hamlet who have money and to spare on overdressing themselves are very few; and vanity is not confined to them or to dress. Southey makes Satan say, in "The Devil's Walk," that:

> "He owned, with a grin,
> That his favourite sin
> Is pride that apes humility."

There is very little of that pride here. Most of the people, instead of aping humility, try to ape aristocracy. And if they cannot ape aristocracy they ape those who are in the grades nearest the aristocracy. Whatever happens, they must play the ape, and in doing so hate anyone who happens to be somewhat original.

It is because of this ape instinct which is so powerful among my parishioners that I have had so much trouble during these past five years.

Because I do not clasp my hands and assume the expression of an expiring saint when I meet people in our village street they hold me up as irreverent. The Creator whom I worship, I feel sure, has no great desire to see the bodies of His creatures always contorted into the classic pose adopted by some of our earlier Christians.

I cannot act the ape even to please my critics. The only act of an ape that I think that I could perform with any skill is to climb a tree. And what would my critics say if their pastor were to do that?

Villagers in their vanity ape the ape in hundreds of ways. The vanity of village weddings is glaring. People with new banking accounts sometimes draw their first cheque so that it shall appear in the local Press that they have given the bride "a cheque" as a wedding-present.

The pride of a bride in her wedding-dress is excusable, almost commendable, as is the pride of the groom in his buttonhole and morning-coat. But what does fill me with loathing is the effort of the two maters and the two paters to see that their son's and their daughter's marriage takes the first place for pomp and ceremony and show among local weddings.

The local reporter is welcomed, and encouraged to make a splash with his account of the magnificent wedding which is being solemnised.

For these events the local clergy are usually too insignificant alone to tie the nuptial knot. A cleric with a name, a title, or a high position in the Church is sought — yea, even implored to come and grace with his presence the great event. And ever afterwards we hear it boasted that someone almost as high as the archangel Gabriel performed the auspicious ceremony.

But the vanity in village weddings palls when we come to the vanity in funerals. At such times, when one would expect to see sorrowing relatives thinking only of their loved one departed, we see instead some thinking only of how best to make the funeral a medium for vulgar display of wealth and rank.

Motor-hearses, several clergymen, fashionable mourning dresses, expensive mourning cards, and, finally, a feast at which all the choicest viands are spread before the sorrowing mourners.

It is my experience that a great sorrow banishes my appetite. I have seen sorrowing men and women gorging themselves after a funeral as though they were eating their Christmas dinner.

When I have watched some of these people, knowing in myself that they were among the biggest and vainest of the scandal-mongers of the locality, I have said silently to myself those lines of Shakespeare in "King Henry VIII.":

"He was a man
Of an unbounded stomach,
ever ranking Himself with princes."

Then I have seen much vanity even at confirmation services. Many proud parents are much more keen on their children's clothes than on their Catechism.

"My Tom or Bill, or Mary or Jane looked much better than So-and-So's Tom or Bill, or Mary or Jane," is a remark that is too frequently overheard; while one hears, alas! too infrequently, any expression of pious hope that the solemn service will help these young people to live noble, Christian lives.

Vanity crops up in our villages again at the baptismal services. We see vain godmothers who had previously refused to be present unless one of their uneuphonious maiden names was branded on the, fortunately, unconscious infant; vain godfathers who promise what they have no intention of performing; and vain parents who label their precious offsprings with some fancy names of a sloppy hero or heroine figuring in a serial story.

Of the vanity of some of our pompous villagers who will only attend a local meeting on condition that they are voted into the chair, or elected to the committee, or specially named as doing good work, I, and most village clergymen, could write columns of disclosures.

Though I feel strongly that some of these should be publicly exposed, I restrain myself. It is not the object of these articles to give personal offence, but to help my fellow-men to a nobler mode of life.

CHAPTER XXIV

ANONYMOUS LETTERS

All men who are in the public eye receive anonymous letters. The Prime Minister, doubtless, receives them by the thousand.

All clergymen and all Nonconformist ministers receive missives from persons who, for some reason or other, prefer to preserve their anonymity.

I have had my share of anonymous letters. Wherever I have laboured these letters have reached me. And when I came to Rusper my anonymous post-bag became so bulky that I seriously considered the enlargement of my letter-box.

Rusper's postman must have a bigger grievance against anonymous letter-writers than has its Rector. I hope the anonymous scribes reward the postman liberally at Christmas-time for the unnecessary work they give him.

He certainly has travelled many a weary mile up and down my twisted drive to deliver those thousands of anonymous letters which have come through the rectory door during my five trying years at Rusper.

They were awaiting me in a heap on the day of my arrival. Every man, clerical or lay, is keen on his correspondence, and I was very eager to open this unusually large bunch of what I hoped would have been letters of welcome.

At first glance I thought that the letters must be intended for my predecessor, as I did not recognise the handwriting on any of the envelopes.

No wonder I did not recognise it! Most of the envelopes were addressed in block capitals, such as a schoolboy might use, others were typed, and one had my name and address cut out of the envelope, apparently with a penknife.

Every care seemed to be taken to assure the absolute anonymity of the writer.

There is one type of envelope that has been coming the rectory way for a long time. It shows a sign of having been folded. Though I am no Sherlock Holmes, I conclude from this that it has, at some stage, been placed in another envelope. This conclusion is strengthened and the reason shown by the fact that the address on it is typewritten, and that it has been posted in the district.

Now, Rusper, progressive though it may be in some ways, does not, so far as I have been able to ascertain, possess a typewriter. Therefore, it seems obvious that this wrapper is addressed in some other part of the country, and is then posted to one of my anonymous parishioners, who then inserts his (or her) latest unsigned message for the Rector, and posts it to me on Wednesday afternoons.

The messages which have been regularly coming to me from this source have usually been written in poetic language. Many of them are excerpts from the major poets.

This "contributor" started with Browning, and selected all the quotations which he (or she) thought applicable to me from the great works of this fine poet.

Then he (or she) passed on to Tennyson, and took me through "In Memoriam," "Morte d'Arthur," "Enoch Arden," "The May-Queen," and then dipped into Shelley.

At the present time he (or she) is busy with Shakespeare. We've done "The Tempest," "The Taming of the Shrew," "Julius Caesar," "Mid-summer Night's Dream," and we are now coursing through "King Lear."

At the present rate of progress we shall have finished Shakespeare by Michaelmas, when we shall probably come on to Masefield, Kipling, and Dr. Bridges. I am very keen on Rupert Brooke's work, and if my contributor will only hurry on to him I shall be very grateful. Possibly he (or she) will be ready to do this when he (or she) learns that my library contains a Shakespeare but no Rupert Brooke.

One of the latest of these excerpts from the poets is the following:

"It is a great sin to swear unto a sin,
But greater sin to keep a sinful oath."

For this quotation I am grateful. Its publication in this book may have some effect upon my anonymous traducers. Perhaps it will be a boomerang, which returning to the sender, will cause him (or her) to apply its meaning to himself (or herself).

Perhaps the most virulent of the anonymous letters that have entered my rectory door was the one that contained the following quotation from Mulock Craik's "Tho Dead Czar:"

"You, foul-tongued
Fanatic or ambitious egotist,
Who thinks God stoops from His high majesty
To lay his finger on your puny head,
And crown it — that you henceforth may parade
Your maggotship throughout the wondering world —
'I am the Lord's anointed.' "

This poor fellow had apparently searched all through the poets to find invective sufficiently scurrilous to hurl it anonymously at his unprotected Rector — and finally had to have recourse to some tirade against a fallen Tsar.

I have heard that some parsons were referred to as village Tsars during tho early Victorian era, but I was tremendously surprised to be likened myself to a ruler of All the Russias. This contributor probably will now bring himself up to date, and we shall soon hear the Rector of Rusper described as the Reverend Lenin Trotsky.

But it is not against the subject matter of the anonymous correspondence that I have received that I make this spirited complaint. What I do protest against is anonymity.

It is not English to send a letter if one is ashamed to sign it. One might expect a tricky Afghan, a wily Turk, or a Prussian Junker to adopt such a backstairs method, but not a healthy-minded Englishman or Englishwoman.

I proudly claim to be a sport. I like to play the game and see the game played. If someone in Rusper, or outside of Rusper, feels that I am not his type of parson — God knows no one can be everyone's ideal type —let him come to my door and say so. If he is honest, I will discuss his grievance with him. And he may change his opinion — and probably will — in five minutes.

But these anonymous letter-writers are not sports. They have never seen the inside of a British public school. They have never been taught what it means to be a Britisher. They are the envious, disgruntled outcasts who have never yet learned their true responsibilities in life.

They are not worth the space that I have already devoted to them. In their sphere I suppose they unwittingly serve a useful purpose — they act as a goad to prevent the righteous from developing swelled head.

Yea, verily, they have kept the head of their Rector from becoming unduly enlarged. For this reason, if for no other, I will try to be grateful to them. And so, dear anonymous writers, I proffer you my thanks.

Chapter XXV

PARISH PIN-PRICKS

To answer some of the grave charges made against me at the Consistory Court was easy compared with dealing with the pin-pricks which came in the daily round and the common task.

Before I had fastened the blinds to my windows or tacked the carpets down on the floors of the rectory, I found that there were some who were trying to thrust pins through the joints of the steel armour which every clergyman finds it necessary to wear.

My first callers asked me what I proposed to do with the school. "My duty, of course!" I replied, not liking their tone. To which they replied that they hoped they would not have to do as they did with my predecessor — drag him out of the house from twiddling his thumbs before the fire.

What manner of people are these? I wondered, as they thus affectionately greeted me. Surely I had struck a new race!

In Thackeray's famous novel, "The Newcomes," is described a Society lady — a great lady, domineering, of the world, worldly. I have found some of these ladies in Rusper.

If I had been a Society clergyman — showy, superficial, like Charles Honeyman, who never sat down in the same trousers in which he walked, who kept in the vestry ungents and perfumes to make himself ridiculous and smell appallingly in the pulpit, and delivered in an affected and artificial manner sententious verbosity; if I described the great doctrine of the Incarnation as the hypostatic union of anthropo-morphised nature, I might have pleased some of these haughty dames, and heard the praise of some village swain that I preached a magnificent sermon, as no word of it could be understood.

One of these ladies arrived at the rectory in great pomp in her motor-car, wearing beautiful white-fox furs, carrying her toy dogs — which safely guarded her fireside by day and the foot of her bed at nights. I was busy writing a sermon for the following Sunday.'

I could see by my visitor's flashing eyes that I had given offence, although I did not then, know why. What did I mean by this gratuitous interference with her servants? she demanded to know. If I did so again she would write to the bishop about it. I am afraid I did not wince as she expected.

Gradually my offence dawned upon me. It appears that I had said to the wife of one of her employés, that even if she had to leave her cottage I would try to find her another; if not, she could take her family to tho rectory, on the second floor, away from the haunted room, which is sacred to a Rusper nun of the sixteenth century. Before her majesty left, I offered her smelling-salts! After she left I threw a plate at the cat!

Another lady attempted to thrust deeply into my armour by neglecting to contribute to the Easter offertory, which dropped from fever heat to zero; other ladies circulated the unfounded rumour that the school children were not being taught Church doctrine. One of them came to see for herself. A few days afterwards I received a letter from the Archdeacon asking me to see him at once.

He told me that he had heard from the parish that I did not teach the children on Sunday afternoons, that the boys and girls made it a practice to run about like wild savages, and that no Church teaching had been given to the children for years. The Archdeacon was too discreet to mention names.

It did not take me long to convince tho worthy Archdeacon that I had never failed to carry out the letter and spirit of the Ecclesiastical Canons, whereby every parson, vicar or curate, is enjoined every Sunday to catechise the children. At the same time I was careful to assert that the teaching was instilled into the children in the most acceptable way, rather than in the harsh manner customary a century ago.

One of the strictures that had been passed upon me was that

I had not prevented boys from bathing in ponds on Sunday afternoons. To chase naked boys out of a pond with a cane, I must confess, I regarded to be the task more for the village schoolmaster than the village parson.

Nevertheless, it was true that some boys who belonged to a City school that were visiting the village had been bathing without permission in a pond in one of my fields. And it was also true that my cows were not too ready to drink from this water for a few days after.

I love the children of Rusper, and the little service which my dear old verger and myself conduct every Sunday afternoon is one of the amenities of my work. I call it the "Cherubs' Service," at which I read, play the music, and catechise.

I write little hymns and tunes, and dedicate them to the children, and they sing the sweet story of old to these new and varied tunes. When the service is over I often play with them in the field.

As I left the Archdeacon I told him that I was afraid in future I should have to enforce the instructions in Canon 19, which runs:

"Loiterers are not to be suffered near the church
at the time of Divine Service."

After all allowances are made, a clergyman, no more than any other man, can be expected to endure too much outside interference with his work. I often wonder what some of these haughty, interfering dames would say if, when they were doing their trivial war work of which they were so proud, I had stopped in and threatened to write to their superiors to say the Sister Susies were not sewing on the buttons on the shirts for soldiers in the proper way; or were wearing their military caps at an unbecoming or unmilitary angle.

One of the biggest of the pin-pricks was the despatch of amateur detectives to Worthing, to London, and to other parishes where I had laboured, to discover if any of the good people of those distant districts had heard or seen anything which would prevent the admission of the new Rector of Rusper to the select circle of our local aristocracy.

They even sent down to Dr. Barnardo's Homes, for whom I used to preach. Someone had started the rumour that I was a Barnardo's boy instead of a Barnardo's preacher. Well, it would never do to have in their houses a man who might have begun life as a waif and stray, however far he had advanced since those early days. So they must send to see.

Another rumour which arose from out the empty void was that I owned a couple of public-houses in London. I would that I did! Within a few weeks from now they would be transformed into dwelling-houses for those cramped and houseless Londoners who are waiting, and always waiting, for the Government houses that never come. Nevertheless, someone dashes up to London on another fruitless mission.

After reading one of those magnificent articles by Mr. Horatio Bottomley, I was once moved to exclaim publicly, "Bottomley is England's lay Archbishop." That exclamation brought its full share of public criticism.

But there is no need to enumerate all the pin-pricks from which I and most village clergymen suffer. They prick him in eating, they prick him in drinking, they prick him in sleeping, they prick him in waking, and they prick him in resting.

Pin-pricks to him are as all-embracing as the curse pronounced on the Jackdaw of Rheims. Fortunately I am almost as impervious to them as was the jackdaw to tho Cardinal's curse.

CHAPTER XXVI

RUSPER'S BRIDGE OF SIGHS

At my college there was a bridge, christened by the students, the Bridge of Sighs, which connected the two wings of the building.

On a landing by one end of this bridge there was posted at regular intervals the results of the examinations. And it was here that many a student read his unlucky fate, and sighed over his failure to impress his pastors and masters.

Rusper, too, has its Bridge of Sighs. It carries the road over a tuneful brook. Here at times sit the rustic lovers, held tightly in the clasp of Cupid.

Here, sometimes, when Cupid was having his half-holiday, have sat succeeding generations of rectors, thinking over the trials of parish work in an isolated village. Sometimes they have discreetly risen and moved away when Cupid, suddenly resuming his sweet duties, has unexpectedly returned to the placid scene.

My immediate predecessor was often seen in this spot. He came to reflect upon the cool stream which sang below, so that it might help him to some isle of the blest where he might forget his parish worries.

One day, in the blaze of noon, when Cupid slept and rustic lovers were ploughing the glebe or boiling the carrots, I arrived at this oasis in a dusty road, and sat down to read for the first time the diary of one of my predecessors.

As I turned the pages I saw an entry which revealed his state of mind as he was delivering Ruspers' now defunct Parish

Magazine.

The residents of two houses were mentioned as no longer desirable people to visit, as they had uttered statements which made it unwise to deliver the magazine at their doors again.

On another page I found a reference to the disbursement of alms money, with the ominous remark:

"Paid from my own pocket £9 7s. 6d., in addition to the alms received for the year. Great God! And some have actually suggested that I misappropriated alms!"

These are only two examples of the malicious things which have been said of those devout men of God who preceded me in Rusper.

All clergymen keep diaries, even as all Bishops keep and have pored over its harrowing contents as I have sat by our Bridge of Sighs.

A few days ago I came across one of the early entries. The leaf was thumb-eared. It told of a private meeting held in some secluded whispering corner of my village, where persons are reported to have resorted to repeat gossips and slanders that they had heard about their Rector.

One of the stories there solemnly related, so says my diary — which cannot lie — was that I had been seen, during morning service, to enter my vestry for my Banns Book. When I returned to the chancel I had been seen to draw my finger across my lips, and the presumption was that I had been drinking the Communion wine.

What a charge! And yet charges of this or a similar nature are often levelled at the clergymen of the Church of England by persons who do not fully realise the gravity of their words.

Another page in my bulging diary reminds me of a glorious day in autumn five years ago, when, after preaching a sermon which had brought me tearful thanks from many a good soul in my congregation, I was approached in the vestry by several persons, who suggested that I was a racing man, a gambler, and owned horses at Newmarket.

In my amateur mind I have a hazy idea that Newmarket thoroughbreds cost thousands — perhaps hundreds of thousands. The most that I have ever spent know of my doubtful successes, not on the racecourse, but on a farm, with these friends of man.

One of my catechisers affirmed that I was seen at a railway-station dressed in loud racing checks. I believe I asked if my interrogators had not seen me actually dressed as a jockey.

My height is something over six feet, and I weigh about fourteen stone. I have heard since that our champion jockey is about half my weight, which explains what I did not then know — the reason why I was not accused of being a professional rider!

Yet another page in my diary reminds me of an accusation that I had refused to bury a man who had just died. Yet the real facts were that not only had I buried this lamented parishioner, but had eulogised him at the graveside, and had actually helped to dig his grave.

I have frequently felt like pitching this diary of false charges and bitter experiences into the babbling brook below me. But as it contains other entries, some of them of loving deeds performed by self-sacrificing Christians in Rusper, I am treasuring it for the time.

Sometimes it burns in my pocket, as did "The Scarlet Letter" on the bosom of that unfortunate heroine in Hawthorne's famous book.

At the present time it is my intention to leave it as a little legacy to my successor, who may will probably be forced to live when he, all unsuspectingly, follows me into this haunt of slander and spiteful tongues.

[Written at the End of the Trial.]

CHAPTER XXVII

HELL BECOMES HEAVEN

There is joy and song in my home to-day; there is music and gladness in my soul. For my five years of hell are over at last!

Those of my readers who have read the daily Press know of what happened at my second trial on April 20th. Not only were the frivolous charges made against me withdrawn, but, I am assured, the campaign of calumny which has been waged against me is definitely at an end.

My wife is twenty years younger, while I am a schoolboy once again. I feel as Job must have felt when his tribulations were over, and those who came to criticise and blame that man of God were confounded, and sought Job's prayers to save them from the wrath of the Most High.

All the week letters of congratulation have been pouring in. So many of my parishioners have come down the drive to my door to shake me by the hand that I shall soon have to invest in many yards of Susan. I had reared this old cow from an orphan calf, had fed her myself from the bucket. She was lost to me during those long, anxious days when everything I possessed had to be disposed of to meet the expenses of my trial. I am afraid that many a sick villager has regretted her disappearance, for Susan used to give the finest milk and the richest cream of any of her kind in the county.

I met Susan at the rectory door on her return in the care of a parishioner. By her calmly happy expression, I felt sure that

Susan must have recognised me again. I hope it will be many a long day before she kicks her last bucket!

My Bishop has joined in the general wave of congratulation; so has Dr. Margaret Tyler, of Highgate, who has presented the church with a £2,000 organ, which shall sound forth the new note that has come into my life, and I trust into the life of all the village.

The church bells rang merrily on the afternoon of my vindication; they have rung merrily ever since. I believe that those strange few who were prepared to run up a flag if I were defeated finally joined in with the general acclamations over my triumph.

In this final installment I would thank all those loyal friends who have stood by me in the day of trial. Though my tribulations were many, though the clouds were low and black, I was ever more fortunate than the Job of Uz. His friends were poor specimans in truth.

My thanks I proffer them now — Church members and Non-conformists, parsons and publicans, saints and sinners, my old colleagues and my new churchwardens, my bell-ringers and the well-wishers who serenaded me after I had returned on the night of my vindication, and all those thousands of persons whom I did not know, but who have written to me letters of good cheer, encouragement, and congratulation.

Of these latter I will give a few extracts. A lady from Crawley writes, stating that "I don't think I should care to be one of your parishioners. I think I should die of shame if I lived in Rusper. May I tell you that there are dozens in Crawley who think you are a brick?"

A vigorous letter comes from Belfort, the writer declaring that:

"You have lit a fire that will stand some putting out, but it will destroy much of the filth and dross that ornaments a large proportion of church-goers."

"I admire your bold stand in exposing the awful ravages that scandal brings," writes a correspondent from Thames Ditton, and proceeds: "I am glad you have had your little 'bit of heaven' amidst the dark, black clouds of calumny. I pray that all these scandalmongers will be deeply convicted by these articles. The arrows of conviction will fly, without a doubt, "going through the mill, and I am fighting hard. I have kept people here in their place with threats of libel actions. Try it — only be sure of your evidence."

A remarkable clever letter written by a young man from Ockley declares that "It is a very great tribute to you to know that men, as a whole, are totally in accord with your views; numberless women, too, can be counted among your supporters. One such declared to me that she felt like patting the Rector of Rusper on the back — and it was meant, too! Nearly every village possesses a gossip celebrity, who magnifies the little episodes into huge proportions."

A correspondent from Norwich states that in his parish an angel would have a very poor chance.

"Would to God we had a few more men like you in our pulpits!" writes a correspondent from Cardiff, and adds: "I am not exactly a Church of England member myself. I don't care where I worship, so long as the preacher is God's man. Our pastor is one like yourself, afraid of nothing, only preaching Christ and Him crucified. Carry on!"

A man and wife jointly sign a letter written from Norbury, which says that "For six years we resided at Crawley, and frequently visited your church, and much enjoyed the services. We write to say how pleased we are that your terrible sufferings are over. Throughout, our confidence in you never wavered, and we join our prayers with yours. You have had many enemies, but you have had friends, too; and although you may not remember us, none are more earnest in their hope for your future peace and happiness."

"I am a discharged wounded soldier, and I appreciate very much the very kind things you have said about others like myself," says another correspondent, whose welcome letter is addressed from Upper Holloway.

"Please accept my sincere sympathy. I only wish I were in a position to defray your expenses," writes an Ashford resident. He says that, from many years of experience, he is convinced that there is no limit to the devilry of some women villagers.

From Holmwood comes a letter written by a young woman, who says that "I have been so interested in your articles, and I am quite longing for the time to come to hear that you have

118

come out with all honours, when you will be able to laugh at your traducers and their idle gossip and scandal. Should there be a fund started on your behalf, I should like to give a little."

"I have read with great delight of your vindication," writes a young lady correspondent from Sussex, and adds: "I know some of those people at Rusper. How I detested their venomous tongues! But, being a woman, I had to bear it."

"These slanderers forget," says a Richmond resident, "that there is a God above taking note of every evil thought and word they utter — a God Who said: 'Vengeance is mine: I will repay.' "

Another well-wisher writes quoting the text: "If ye were of the world, the world would love its own: because ye are not of the world, therefore the world hates you."

From Ockley, Surrey, comes a very outspoken letter, in which the writer says: "Courageous you certainly must be, and your revelations are remarkably true. Your outspoken words will, I honestly believe, contribute in some measure to this end, and your indomitable will and determination is generally admired."

And still another writes:

"I knew that you would win in the end. Your experiences must have filled thousands with indignation, and also, I must confess, it amused thousands. My friends and I have screamed over some of the funny paragraphs — particularly over the Jumble Sale article."

As the result of numerous letters from clergymen who have urged me to continue my campaign against village gossip in the interest of the profession, I have decided to form a society which shall undertake the defence of clergymen who, like myself, are forced into the courts to defend their good name. I trace many of my troubles to an Act of Parliament passed in 1892, which omits to insist that, before permitting a public trial of a clergyman, the Bishop shall first arrange a private inquiry to see if there are *prima facie* grounds for allowing a clergyman's name to be dragged through the mud. In my own case, the Bishop did not make inquiries from me; if it had been compulsory for him to do so, much of my five years of hell would have been obviated. My churchwardens and I had two interviews with my Bishop, it is true. At the first interview the Bishop declared that he did not believe a word of what was alleged, and at the second he said: "Synnott, you are a man; go and fight it!"

I fought, and won; but it ought never to have been possible to compel me to fight such an objectionable case. I have been vindicated, it is true, but the fact that persons once slung mud at me will always be remembered by all who have heard of the Rector of Rusper.

However, it is all over now. To those who have stood by me in the supreme test I offer my thanks; to those thoughtless or malicious persons who have slandered me I extend the hand of forgiveness, even as I hope myself to be forgiven. Some have already come to me like men, confessed their mistake, and are numbered again among my congregation. I am glad to see them back. I will welcome gladly all others who come, and will say to them, "Let the dead past bury its dead."

Meanwhile, I take comfort from the fact that though I have gone through the Valley of the Shadow for five years, though I have been sacrificed upon the altar of the Consistory Court, this terrible experience may still be of benefit to those thirty-six thousand other clergymen in the Church of England, and countless more, who now suffer, or might have been made to suffer, from the evil tongues of the calumniator. With renewed courage and unshaken faith, I bring these chapters to an end, and in my quiet parish of Rusper prepare to enter upon a period of which, a few years hence... I may be able to write under the revised title — "Five Years' *Heaven* in a Country Parish."